revolution

GEORGE BARNA

TYNDALE HOUSE PUBLISHERS, INC., CAROL STREAM, ILLINOIS

BARNA

Visit Tyndale's exciting Web site at www.tyndale.com

TYNDALE is a registered trademark of Tyndale House Publishers, Inc.

Tyndale's quill logo is a trademark of Tyndale House Publishers, Inc.

Barna and the Barna logo are trademarks of George Barna.

BarnaBooks is an imprint of Tyndale House Publishers, Inc.

Revolution

Designed by Dean H. Renninger

Library of Congress Cataloging-in-Publication Data

Barna, George.
  Revolution / George Barna.
    p. cm.
  ISBN-13: 978-1-4143-0758-9 (hardcover)
  ISBN-10: 1-4143-0758-6 (hardcover)
  1. Church renewal. 2. Church. I. Title.
  BV600.2.B343 2005
  277.3'083—dc22   2005016242

ISBN-13: 978-1-4143-1016-9 (hardcover - George Barna Ed.)
ISBN-10: 1-4143-1016-1 (hardcover - George Barna Ed.)

Printed in the United States of America

11 10 09 08 07 06
7   6   5   4

Contents

SOON AFTER GRADUATING from Boston College, I took a job as a policy analyst in the Massachusetts legislature. The experience and contacts gained from that position evolved into campaign management for a variety of candidates running for federal and state offices. One of the most captivating aspects of those positions was the art of estimating the future and figuring out how to prepare people for what was coming. After more education and additional years in the trenches of political and marketing activity, my wife and I opened the Barna Research Group. That platform allowed me to work with—and learn important lessons from—an array of clients that spanned the gamut from media powerhouses such as Disney and ABC to organizations as diverse as Visa and the military, as well as numerous Christian ministries. The research became a springboard from which to consider the future and the most strategic responses to emerging possibilities.

After completing a substantial amount of research exploring society from various angles, I wrote a book in 1990 titled *The Frog in the Kettle*. The premise was that we could predict what would happen in the United States during the coming decade with reasonable accuracy, enabling individuals and organizations—including Christian ministries—to anticipate changes, help shape them, and capitalize upon the transitioning nature of our culture. It is rewarding to look back on the content of the book and realize that more than 90 percent of the predicted outcomes became reality. The most gratifying results, though, were the statements of many leaders who indicated that such forward thinking had helped their ministries thrive amidst chaos and difficulty.

The book you are holding provides an even more significant description of the intersection of cultural change and spiritual transformation. Unlike *The Frog in the Kettle*, this is not a book about a myriad of trends. It is a book about a single trend that is already redefining faith and the Church in our country. It is about an explosion of spiritual energy and activity we are calling the Revolution—an unprecedented reengineering of America's faith dimension that is likely to be the most significant transition in the religious landscape that you will ever experience. As you read the chapters that follow, you will understand why I make such a bold claim.

Let me explain why I wrote this book. There are three outcomes that I hope to accomplish. First, I want to inform people of the radical changes that are reshaping the Church in America. Using our nationwide research, along with narratives offered by many Revolutionaries about their spiritual journey, as the foundation, this book is intended to paint a picture of the existing state of the Revolution and where it is headed.

Second, beyond simply introducing the Revolution and its participants, I desire to help Revolutionaries gain a better understanding of themselves. Many of them feel like the odd person out, and most of them struggle with conflicting feelings about their status as spiritual champions who have no spiritual homeland. What a joy it would be if this slim volume helped to crystallize their self-awareness, legitimize their commendable quest to be Christlike, and provide some clarifying language and practical resources to assist them on their journey.

Finally, I want to encourage people who are struggling with their place in the Kingdom of God to consider this spiritual awakening as a viable alternative to what they have pursued and experienced thus far. Sometimes people know what they want and need to do, but feel constrained by circumstances or expectations. May this book provide those people with the permission they need to reach their next level of spiritual maturity.

Whether you want to or not, you will have to take a stand in regard to the Revolution. It is on track to become the most significant recalibration of the American Christian body in more than a century. Your response ought not be based on whether you are comfortable with it, but rather on its consistency with biblical principles and its capacity to advance the Kingdom of God. If you are a follower of Jesus Christ, then you must understand this Revolution of faith because it is already impacting your life, and it will continue to do so in the years to come. It is my prayer that this book will provide the insights you need to comprehend this spiritual dynamic and discover how your own faith voyage is—or should be—linked to the Revolution.

And, if you discover that you are—or want to become—a Revolutionary, welcome to the fold.

As a practical matter, be forewarned that throughout this

book I use the words *church* (small *c*) and *Church* (capital *C*) in very different ways. The distinction is critical. The small *c* church refers to the congregation-based faith experience, which involves a formal structure, a hierarchy of leadership, and a specific group of believers. The term *Church*, on the other hand, refers to all believers in Jesus Christ, comprising the population of heaven-bound individuals who are connected by their faith in Christ, regardless of their local church connections or involvement. Some hail this as the Church universal, as opposed to the church local. As you will see, the Revolution is designed to advance the Church and to redefine the church.

You might feel relieved and excited by the content of this book—or you might respond with intense anger or disapproval. Whatever you feel, I ask that you read the entire book before you pass judgment on it. The book is neither long nor theologically dense; it is a "fast read." But it is meant to be a cohesive and complete argument that benefits from a full and open-minded hearing.

Thank you for giving me the opportunity to share some of the challenging and life-transforming realities that have changed millions of Americans. I am honored and humbled to admit that I am now counted among that crowd.

Abundant blessings to you,

George Barna
VENTURA, CALIFORNIA
JUNE 2005

I WOULD LIKE TO THANK the following individuals, each of whom has played a unique and significant role in the development of this book.

My colleagues in The Barna Group have helped me in a variety of ways. I am honored to serve with this team in the trenches of day-to-day ministry. Thank you to Thom Black, Cameron Hubiak, Pam Jacob, David Kinnaman, Jamie McLaughlin, and Celeste Rivera. Thom has worked particularly closely with me on developing this aspect of our ministry. His insights, encouragement, and friendship have been invaluable.

My friends at Tyndale House Publishers have helped me to shape the communication of this message and to get the information into the hands of many people. I have especially benefited from my interaction with Doug Knox and Jan Long Harris, but I am grateful for the efforts of the many people involved on their team.

Helpful reactions have been provided by friends and colleagues before, during, and after the manuscript development phase. I am so grateful for the ideas and insights provided by Henry Blackaby, Mark Hatch, Mark Holmen, Chuck Laird, Gabe Lyons, Kevin Mannoia, Doug Murren, Alan Nelson, Steve Russo, James Ryle, John Saucier, Jay Strack, Tim Tassopoulos, and Glenn Terrell. They are not responsible for the content herein; in fact, a few of them are rather dismayed by the content. Regardless, I am appreciative of the wisdom and grace they shared with me, even when our perspectives were miles apart. If there is any blame due in response to this material, spare them your wrath; they are not responsible for the contents.

This book is about Revolutionaries, and it is their example that has instigated this book and helped to transform my own spiritual journey. As Thom Black and I have crossed the country interviewing and interacting with Revolutionaries, we have been deeply challenged and moved by the faith of these men and women. My sincere thanks are extended to each of you for your integrity and diligence in showing me and others what it means to love God and people with all your heart, mind, strength, and soul.

My family has supported me in my lurching quest to be a faithful and fruitful servant of God. They know, firsthand, how often I miss the target. But they continue to humor me, challenge me, support me, and love me. My wife, Nancy, has put up with my antics for more than three decades. My daughters, Samantha and Corban, are a constant source of joy and strength. Thank you, all three of you, for continuing to love me, even when my activities on behalf of the Church seem crazy. I pray that God will bless you many times over.

In many respects, this is a love letter to the One who suffered and died for me. Jesus, may Your Kingdom be honored and advanced by the ideas and call to action put forth in this book. It is my privilege to know, love, and serve You.

chapter one

> DAVID AND MICHAEL

THE SUN WAS ALREADY heating up the morning air, drying the dew on the clipped grass at the sixth hole of the Winston Estates Country Club golf course. Two men in their mid-thirties were reveling in the beauty of the day and the pure enjoyment of playing the sport they loved. For one of them, this was usually the highlight of the week.

With his head down and his eyes focused on the ball, David slowly swung his two-wood back and forth behind the tiny white sphere nestled on the tee. He then took a full swing and launched the puckered ball a good 250 yards down the middle of the fairway. Grinning with competitive confidence, he turned to his companion and challenged him. "Beat that, Mr. Long Ball!"

Michael grinned and brushed past his friend, jammed a gold-plated tee into the turf, and placed his ball atop the tiny holder. Taking a few moments to get lined up and ready, he sprang into his swing, smacking the ball as hard as he could. Both men stood silent for a few seconds, watching as the miniscule white speck sliced through the air, getting smaller and smaller before it hit the ground and rolled to a stop just a few feet from David's ball—a few feet *past* it.

Looking David in the eye, Michael pursed his lips and quietly replied, "Challenge accepted. Mission accomplished." He playfully shoved David out of his path as they retreated to the edge of the fairway to retrieve their golf bags. Both men laughed as they shouldered their bags and trekked across the manicured lawn toward their next swing.

The duo had known each other for more than a decade, initially meeting at a church barbecue. There were many similarities in their lives: each had two daughters (who were roughly the same age), each was the CEO of a midsized corporation experiencing solid growth, each got married to a loving and supportive wife soon after graduating from college, and both were born-again Christians who had eliminated church life from their busy schedules, albeit with very different subsequent paths.

Initially they took identical steps of disengagement. Driven out of their longtime church by boredom and the inability to serve in ways that made use of their considerable skills and knowledge, each man spent some time exploring other churches. After months of honest effort, neither found a ministry that was sufficiently stimulating and having an impact on the surrounding community. David, entrepreneurial to a fault, decided to develop his own regimen of spiritual practices and activities in order to retain a vibrant spiritual life. Michael, disheartened by his unfulfilled quest, chose to call a truce with God and simply get on with life, sans church.

The businessmen unexpectedly reconnected some time later at a business function. Upon discovering their similar frustrations in trying to find a satisfying spiritual home, they sought an opportunity to get together and continue their conversation. That task revealed that the only overlapping gap in their schedules was Sunday mornings. And thus the "Church on the Green," as they jokingly referred to their biweekly rendezvous, was born.

David and Michael thought of themselves as "deeply spiritual" people. Their irregular attendance at church services—each attended on occasion with their families, who remained more or less regulars at a nearby church—failed to dampen their enthusiasm for God. They believed that the Bible is God's true and reliable Word for life. They each gave money generously to causes they felt were trustworthy and significantly helped people. They prayed before meals and had shared a number of stories with each other about how pastors and other Christians had chastised them for their failure to be involved in church life.

Although both men thought of themselves as Christians and were considered by those who knew them best to be ethical and decent human beings, their spiritual trajectories were far from identical.

"Look at those mountains over there," David entreated his friend as they marched toward their next spot on the fairway. "They are absolutely stunning, don't you think?" He stopped for a moment and wistfully stared at the evergreen-covered landmass rising high above the course. "Awesome," he exclaimed loudly, hurrying to catch up with his determined compatriot. "Every time I see them my batteries get recharged. God's handiwork gets to me every time. Aren't they something?" Michael grunted a sign of agreement but seemed more intent upon adding up their scores through the first half-dozen holes. His indifference did not deter David.

"Hey, remember I was telling you a couple of weeks ago about that short-term missions trip I signed up our family for, the one in Central America scheduled for this fall? Well, I called the lady running the event and talked to her about the needs of the people we'd be serving down there. She had all kinds of great ideas, and I decided to see if I could get the prayer group at work to fund a pallet of clothes we could send in advance of our arrival." David was talking faster now, excited about the project he was describing. "It doesn't cost that much, and it'd make a huge difference in their lives, especially the kids down there. I wanted to give the others at work a chance to participate in it, so we're pooling some money to cover the costs. I've got a couple of people supervising the purchasing and shipping. You want in on this?"

Michael glanced at his longtime friend, shook his head with a grin, and said, "Yup, that's you, Mr. You-Got-Problems-I-Got-Solutions. Sure, why not, put me down for whatever you think makes sense. You still slinging hash in the serving line down at the homeless shelter every week?"

David nodded his affirmation and added, "It's part of my someday-to-be-ex-CEO social reentry plan. I want to be sure that when the board fires me I have alternatives lined up."

The duo laughed at David's self-effacing comment before he continued. "By the way, Michael, remind me to give you a book I have in the car that I've been saving for you. It's been really helpful to me, and I thought about you when I read it. It's about biblical principles on leadership. It challenged me, so I know it'll be a challenge to you."

Again, both men playfully slapped at each other before Michael drew a four-iron from his bag, tossed the case on the ground at his partner's feet, and lightly threw down the gauntlet as well. "Now, tell me, you don't honestly think you're gonna take me on this hole, do you?"

Two minutes later, after hitting their approach shots, the pair strode toward the green to get in their final strokes on the hole. En route, David picked up the conversation.

"You read anything revealing in the Bible lately?"

Michael glanced at his partner and sighed. "Man, with the merger and that big board meeting coming up, I've been lucky to eat, much less read the Book. How about you?"

David's face took on a ponderous look. "Oh, you know how it is, there's so much. I think this past week the big insight for me was in Romans 11, the part that says we have nothing to lose by living in flagrant opposition to the world. It can strip us of our stuff, but it can never remove God's anointing and blessings. We can only lose His favor willfully—by choosing to turn our back on God and His Kingdom and pursuing other outcomes besides those He calls us to. I guess I felt a new sense of release to passionately seek holiness amidst the opposition of the world, remembering that I can lose only if I abandon my focus on God. It's also affected my relationship with Bill, that guy in shipping whom I befriended after his wife and kids left him. He really needs

Jesus, but he's been hurt by the church before, so I've been trying to take things slowly with him. As always," he summarized, "God seems to know just what I need when I need it, and studying Romans has been so helpful for me."

Michael acknowledged the importance of David's words but seemed distracted. Challenged by David, the younger of the two believers admitted, "You know, I focus on my faith as much as I can, but it's a struggle, you know that. All the pressures—the office, home, community responsibilities, my health—man, I marvel that you find time to squeeze in some Bible and all the outreach stuff you do. No matter what I've said about you publicly, you're really a pretty decent guy."

David mockingly smacked his peer across the head, disturbing the perfect alignment of his hair. "You meathead, your faith needs to be a priority, not an add-on. That's what you never seem to get. It's not about trying to shoehorn God into your packed schedule; it's about building your schedule around Him. That's a whole different perspective, my man, a whole different perspective."

Michael appeared to be reflecting on those words when David changed the subject. "Hey, I almost forgot. The wife wanted me to invite you and your clan over next week to celebrate Jenny's birthday. We're having friends over, but you're welcome, too. During one of our family prayer times last week, Joelle felt as if the Lord wanted us to have you guys join the festivities. Must be a sign from the Lord that He still loves you, you unremorseful backslider." David jumped back just as Michael teasingly swung his club at the taller man's midsection.

"Birthday party?" yelled Michael in mock astonishment. "That's something the heathens do. How the mighty have fallen, O holy one of God. But sure. Free food and drink? Count us in." He looked over the fairway, took a deep breath of the clean morning air, and flashed a toothy grin at his buddy. "Now, get ready to pay homage to the true king of the fairway. This baby's rollin' to center cup. Move over, amateur, and take notes on how it's done."

‡

You probably know people like David and Michael. You might even be like one of them. David, you see, is a Revolutionary Christian. His life reflects the very ideals and principles that characterized the life and purpose of Jesus Christ and that advance the Kingdom of God—despite the fact that David rarely attends church services. He is typical of a new breed of disciples of Jesus Christ. They are not willing to play religious games and aren't interested in being part of a religious community that is not intentionally and aggressively advancing God's Kingdom. They are people who want more of God—much more—in their lives. And they are doing whatever it takes to get it.

Michael, for all his good qualities and wonderful intentions, is a "backsliding" Christian—a believer who is losing touch with God, the Bible, the community of faith, and his spiritual responsibilities. That's easy to do in our society: so many distractions and alternatives confront us every day, it's miraculous that anyone even remembers God. But Michael's

frustration with life can ultimately be traced to his willingness to become a spiritual victim rather than a spiritual warrior. He loves God, has prayed that Jesus Christ would save
him from his sins, and believes many biblical doctrines. But
Michael's life is more about living for Michael than it is
about living for God.

The United States is home to an increasing number of
Revolutionaries. These people are devout followers of Jesus
Christ who are serious about their faith, who are constantly
worshipping and interacting with God, and whose lives are
centered on their belief in Christ. Some of them are aligned
with a congregational church, but many of them are not.
The key to understanding Revolutionaries is not what
church they attend, or even if they attend. Instead, it's their
complete dedication to being thoroughly Christian by view-
ing every moment of life through a spiritual lens and making
every decision in light of biblical principles. These are individuals who are determined to glorify God every day
through every thought, word, and deed in their lives.

This book is about the new breed of Christian Revolutionaries emerging in America and the spiritual Revolution
they are bringing with them.

chapter two

> THE REVOLUTIONARY AGE

A QUIET REVOLUTION is rocking the nation. The media are oblivious to it. Scholars are clueless about it. The government caught a glimpse of it in the 2004 presidential election but has mostly misinterpreted its nature and motivations. And Christian churches are only vaguely aware that something seems different, but they have little idea what it's all about.

Let me be the first to welcome you to the Revolutionary Age. The community of faith has instigated many ages in the past. Church history recounts such times as the Apostolic Age, the Time of the Martyrs, the era of the Desert Fathers, the Period of the Mystics, the Reformation, the Great Awakening, and the Missionary Age, to name a few.

Today, we have the Revolutionary Age. It fits our cultural context, doesn't it? Newspapers, magazines, and television shows belch out endless stories about the information revolution, the technological revolution, the sexual revolution, the globalization revolution, the entrepreneurial revolution, the conservative revolution, and so forth. It's amazing that most people are totally unaware of the most important renaissance of them all: the spiritual revolution that is reshaping Christianity, personal faith, corporate religious experience, and the moral contours of the nation.

DEFINING OUR TERMS

We live in an era of hyperbole. Everything is supersized, global, mega-this, and biggest-ever-that. Even the religious community has succumbed to the world's infatuation with size. The pinnacle of church success is to become a megachurch. The ultimate in presentations is to have a big-screen projection system. Evangelism has traded in tent revivals for stadium crusades. Televangelists have moved beyond network broadcasting to satellite feeds that reach every nation in the world. Faithful mom-and-pop Christian bookstores are closing by the hundreds because Christian publishers have placed their products in the "big box" retailers, such as Wal-Mart, Costco, Target, and Barnes & Noble.

Revolution is one of those "big ideas" that has caught fire among marketers. In recent years they have capitalized on the word, hoping to generate the almighty street buzz by exploiting the dangerous feel of the term—often as a means of distracting consumers from the absence of an edgy product. So Chevrolet trumpets its "revolution" while selling the same old vehicles with slicker advertising and a few bells and whistles. A group of executives leave their positions at major movie studios to form an independent production company, named Revolution Studios, to develop relatively mainstream films, many of which fall far short of the distinctiveness promised by the company's name. (Remember the universally panned film *Gigli*?) The Green Revolution is an uninspiring approach to eradicating world hunger through the use of high-yield agricultural techniques of dubious performance. The Nintendo Revolution is simply the marketing label attached to the latest generation of video games from the giant game maker.

Webster, not one to succumb to societal pressure to exaggerate, defines a revolution as "an overthrow or repudiation and thorough replacement of an established government or political system by the people governed." It adds that a revolution may also be a "radical and pervasive change in society and the social structure."

Webster is aptly describing the transformation occurring in American spirituality today. Millions of devout followers of Jesus Christ are repudiating tepid systems and practices of the Christian faith and introducing a wholesale shift in how faith is understood, integrated, and influencing the world. Because human beings become what they believe, and practicing what they believe is the swiftest and surest means of generating lasting change, this revolution of faith is the most significant transition you or I will experience during our lifetime.

Hmm, does that sound as if I'm the one who is now guilty of hyperbole? I don't think so.

WHY NOW?

One of the hallmarks of this period of history is the unprecedented busyness of people's lives. More responsibilities and distractions bombard the typical American than anyone would have imagined possible just a century ago. It is in the midst of this cultural context—a society defined by seemingly infinite opportunities and options and supported by a worldview best summarized by a single word: *whatever*—that this countercultural, faith-based response has emerged.

In essence, our culture's inability to provide fulfillment has caused millions of individuals—who are serious about understanding their existence and living right—to live in a manner that never fails to raise eyebrows in a society that is notably shockproof and dispassionate. These people have chosen to live in concert with core biblical principles. That strategic choice makes them stand out as extremists in a culture that keeps pushing the boundaries of extremism. These are the true Revolutionaries.

What makes Revolutionaries so startling is that they are confidently returning to a first-century lifestyle based on faith, goodness, love, generosity, kindness, simplicity, and other values deemed "quaint" by today's frenetic and morally untethered standards. This is not the defeatist retreat of an underachieving, low-capacity mass of people. It is an intelligent and intentional embrace of a way of life that is the only viable antidote to the untenable moral standards, dysfunctional relationships, material excess, abusive power, and unfortunate misapplication of talent and knowledge that pass for life in America these days. Many Revolutionaries have tested the alternatives and found them to be woefully inadequate. Now, like children who sheepishly realize that Mama was right all along, they have gratefully and humbly accepted the opportunity to do what is right, simply because it is right, even if it is not original or culturally hip.

The unfortunate truth is that most citizens of "the greatest nation on earth" are mired in an agonizing revolving door of trial-and-error efforts in a disheartening and unfulfilling search for truth, integrity, meaning, wholeness, connection, passion, and inner peace. Being in the presence of people who seem to have discovered the keys to achieving such lofty and desirable outcomes cannot help but cause earnest seekers to take notice—and to wonder how it is even remotely possible for Revolutionaries to succeed in our sophisticated age with such simple values and practices.

CONVENTIONAL PRACTICES ARE THE CORNERSTONES

As we journey together, I want to show you what our research has uncovered regarding a growing sub-nation of people, already well over 20 million strong, who are what we call Revolutionaries.

What "established systems" are they seeking to "overthrow or repudiate" and "thoroughly replace," in Webster's words?

They have no use for churches that play religious games, whether those games are worship services that drone on without the presence of God or ministry programs that bear no spiritual fruit. Revolutionaries eschew ministries that compromise or soft sell our sinful nature to expand organizational turf. They refuse to follow people in ministry leadership positions who cast a personal vision rather than God's, who seek popularity rather than the proclamation of truth in their public statements, or who are more concerned about their own legacy than that of Jesus Christ. They refuse to donate one more dollar to man-made monuments that mark their own achievements and guarantee their place in history. They are unimpressed by accredited degrees and endowed chairs in Christian colleges and seminaries that produce young people incapable of defending the Bible or unwilling to devote their lives to serving others. And Revolutionaries are embarrassed by language that promises Christian love and holiness but turns out to be all sizzle and no substance.

In fact, many Revolutionaries have been active in good churches that have biblical preaching, people coming to Christ and being baptized, a full roster of interesting classes and programs, and a congregation packed with nice people. There is nothing overtly wrong with anything taking place at such churches. But Revolutionaries innately realize that it is just not enough to go with the flow. The experience provided through their church, although better than average, still seems flat. They are seeking a faith experience that is more robust and awe inspiring, a spiritual journey that prioritizes transformation at every turn, something worthy of the Creator whom their faith reflects. They are seeking the spark provided by a commitment to a true revolution in thinking, behavior, and experience, where settling for what is merely good and above average is defeat.

Revolutionaries zealously pursue an intimate relationship with God, which Jesus Christ promised we could have through Him. They recognize that there is a huge price to pay in this lifetime—but they are mindful of the eternal payoff as well. Faced with an abundance of options, Revolutionaries make their decisions with great care, knowing that each choice matters to God.

In America today, the easiest thing to get away with is going with the flow. The ride is smoother and resistance is minimized. But like the wide path that Scripture warns most people will take, it is a comfortable route that eventually and inevitably results in disaster. To the Revolutionary, there is no such thing as "going along to get along." You either stand for Jesus or you stand for all that He died to repudiate. To the Revolutionary, yes indeed, life truly is that simple, it is that black-and-white, whether university scholars and the media ridicule that point of view or not. After all, they are not the ultimate Judge to whom we will all give account someday. And it is only that Judge's pronouncement that matters.

In this book I will describe what The Barna Group has learned about this under-the-radar but seminal renaissance of faith that will remake the religious contours of this country over the coming quarter-century. You will find out about the seven spiritual passions that fuel the growth of Revolutionaries. You will read about the mentality and the courage of these pioneers as they risk image, resources, and security to be more attentive to and compliant with the God who means everything to them. And you will be invited to look deep into your own heart and soul to identify your place on the spiritual continuum. Perhaps you, too, have the makings of a spiritual Revolutionary—and the desire to participate in this moment of profound change.

COUNT THE COST

Revolutionaries invariably turn to God's Word—the Bible—for their guidance. In that vein, I encourage you to take heed of Jesus' admonition to His followers always to "count the cost" of choices you make, especially the choice to be a full-on, no-holds-barred follower of His.

Know this: just as the prophets of old were unwelcome in their own hometown, so are Revolutionaries looked at askance by even their closest friends and family members. The skepticism of those who lead conventional spiritual lives is a palpable reminder that growth always comes with a price tag.

Be forewarned: just as Jesus Christ, the ultimate lover of humanity, was scorned, misunderstood, persecuted, and eventually murdered for His extreme love, goodness, compassion, humility, wisdom, and grace, so are Revolutionaries abused by a culture that is itself in crisis. The mere presence of Revolutionaries makes the typical American citizen—yes, even the typical churchgoer—uncomfortable. It is not uncommon for Revolutionaries to meet with rejection—verbal, intellectual, relational, or experiential—simply because of their determination to honor the God they love.

You have probably heard about the "culture war" that rages in the United States today. Perhaps the most significant battle in that war will be waged by the Revolutionaries. They are entrenched at ground zero in the test of wills and worldviews that is shaking our nation. Like their role model, Jesus Christ, they ignite fierce resistance merely by being present and holy. It is perhaps that holy presence that will get Revolutionaries in the deepest trouble they will face—and that will bring lasting healing to a culture that has rebelled for too long against its loving Creator. These Christian zealots are radically reshaping both American society and the Christian Church. Their legacy is likely to be a spiritual reformation of unprecedented proportions in the United States, and perhaps the world.

Are you a Revolutionary? Is someone in your family or your circle of friends a Revolutionary? Would you like to be a Revolutionary—someone who lives only to love, obey, and serve God, rejecting and overcoming every obstacle that emerges to prevent such a life? Read on. . . .

chapter three

> WHAT DOES GOD EXPECT?

THE TENDENCY OF MANY PEOPLE —especially those who are skeptical of the spiritual integrity of and biblical grounds for the emerging faith transformation—will be to dismiss Revolutionaries because such individuals and their faith practices are allegedly not in full compliance with Scripture. That concern is a valid consideration; every person who embraces the name *Christian* and seeks to live in ways that honor Jesus Christ must be willing to evaluate everything in light of what the Bible teaches.

But at the same time we must take God's words to Peter to heart: "Do not call something unclean if God has made it clean" (Acts 11:9). We must be very careful how we critique another person's spiritual journey. If someone's path conforms to biblical guidelines—even though it may stray from church traditions, cultural expectations, or our personal comfort zone—then we must accept the possibility that God may be working through him or her in a manner that is different from how He is working through us, or perhaps different from the ways we have previously seen or experienced

His leading. We are called to be wise and discerning, but not judgmental.

In other words, we are not called to judge the spiritual path of other believers who are dedicated to pleasing God and blessing people when the root of our concern is their style or approach, even though they are true to biblical principles and commands. We are to be discerning in our observation of how fellow believers connect with God and respond to His exhortations, and sensitive to the latitude He has allowed us within the boundaries of Scripture.

WHAT THE BIBLE SAYS

Since the Bible is the source of motivation and wisdom in our efforts to be more Christlike, let's examine the key biblical passages regarding the nature of the Church—that is, the aggregation of followers of Jesus Christ whom He has saved. The most pertinent passages are in the book of Acts, which describes the life of the early Church, immediately after Jesus returned to heaven and allowed the leaders He had trained to develop the Church.

> *All the believers devoted themselves to the apostles' teaching, and to fellowship, and to sharing in meals (including the Lord's supper), and to prayer. A deep sense of awe came over them all, and the apostles performed many miraculous signs and wonders. And all the believers met together in one place and shared everything they had. They sold their property and possessions and shared the money with those in*

need. They worshiped together at the Temple each day, met in homes for the Lord's Supper, and shared their meals with great joy and generosity—all the while praising God and enjoying the goodwill of all the people. And each day the Lord added to their fellowship those who were being saved. (ACTS 2:42-47)

All the believers lifted their voices together in prayer. . . . After this prayer, the meeting place shook, and they were all filled with the Holy Spirit. Then they preached the word of God with boldness. All the believers were united in heart and mind. And they felt that what they owned was not their own, so they shared everything they had. The apostles testified powerfully to the resurrection of the Lord Jesus, and God's great blessing was upon them all. There were no needy people among them, because those who owned land or houses would sell them and bring the money to the apostles to give to those in need. (ACTS 4:24, 31-35)

The high priest and his officials, who were Sadducees, were filled with jealousy. They arrested the apostles and put them in the public jail. . . . Then they brought the apostles before the high council, where the high priest confronted them. "Didn't we tell you never again to teach in this man's name?" he demanded. . . . But Peter and the apostles replied, "We must obey God rather than any human authority. . . ." [The council] called in the apostles and had them flogged. Then they ordered them never again to speak in the name of Jesus, and they let them go. The apostles left

the high council rejoicing that God had counted them worthy to suffer disgrace for the name of Jesus. And every day, in the Temple and from house to house, they continued to teach and preach this message: "Jesus is the Messiah."
(Acts 5:17-18, 27-29, 40-42)

THE SEVEN PASSIONS OF REVOLUTIONARIES

Wow! I would *love* to be involved in a ministry like that, wouldn't you? That's what the Revolution is all about: making it possible to live in such a way, in connection with other like-minded people, that the description we just read is not merely an artifact of Christian history, but a depiction of our Christian experience today.

What made the early Church, which I believe God designed to be our model, compelling and life changing? Let's identify some of the attributes that made the first Church so attractive and effective. If you study these passages and categorize their content, you find that the Church was characterized by seven core passions.

Intimate Worship

Every believer was expected to worship God every day, both in private and in the company of other believers. This did not require a "worship service"; it only necessitated a commitment to feel the awe of God's magnificence, to express gratitude for His love and authority, to acknowledge His control and power, to follow Him with dedication, and to enjoy the miracle of His relationship with us.

Faith-Based Conversations

Just as Jesus was intractable in His pursuit of us, we are called upon to share His love with those who have not yet understood it or embraced it. It is natural to talk about and promote the things that excite us. Nothing should excite us more than the realization that God Himself loves us, wants an intimate relationship with us, and allows us to invite others into that sacred and priceless relationship with Him. The evangelistic efforts of the first believers were carried out through preaching, low-key/high-impact conversations about truth and purpose, prayer, performing miracles to foster the opportunity to discuss the Source of their power, and the joy-filled perspective they had toward God and life that created interest in their lives.

Intentional Spiritual Growth

The Church in Jerusalem endeavored to learn more about the Christian faith and employ the principles of Jesus' teaching. Believers exhibited a remarkable attitude toward life and people and acknowledged the presence of the supernatural in their everyday adventures. They placed their faith at the center of their lives and derived their sense of meaning, purpose, and direction from their connection to God and His commands.

Servanthood

Love is more than a feeling; it is a tangible reality when it is shared with other people through acts of selfless service. The early Church fostered the notion that serving other people was the best means of demonstrating the example that Jesus had set for them. Servanthood also showed the transformation that their faith had wrought within them. Like Christ, they lived to serve rather than to be served.

Resource Investment

Because we own nothing in this life, it is best to wisely invest the resources we manage for the One who is the true owner of all things. The first Christians defined communal living through their sacrificial sharing of everything they had. Note that the Scriptures specifically tell us that they shared "everything" with those in need, and that they used the variety of resources at their disposal—money, food, clothing, housing, relationships, influence, skills, time—for the benefit of all believers.

Spiritual Friendships

The Church was all about relationships. These friends of Jesus became friends with each other and reveled in their mutual admiration of Christ in their frequent get-togethers. The friendships they formed provided not only encouragement but also loving accountability for spiritual integrity.

Family Faith

Christian families taught the ways of God in their homes every day. Parents were expected to model a Spirit-led lifestyle for their children, and families were to make their home a sanctuary for God. In a very real sense, the home *was* the early Church—supplemented by larger gatherings in the

Temple and elsewhere, but never replaced by what took place in the homes of believers.

It is the persistent exercise of these seven passions that makes Revolutionaries just what their name implies. They are not perfect people, and they are not always the best example of genuine Christian behavior. But they are obsessed with becoming just that.

THE FRUIT OF THE EFFORT

One of the most important lessons I've learned from studying the words of Jesus is that He loved fruit. Not the kind you pick off trees or vines, but the kind that's evident in the life of a person whom He has changed. He made very clear that the proof of people's faith is not in the information they know or the religious gatherings they attend, but in the way they integrate what they know and believe into their everyday practices.

The hallmarks of the Church that Jesus died for are clear, based on Scripture: your profession of faith in Christ must be supported by a lifestyle that provides irrefutable evidence of your complete devotion to Jesus. The Lord encountered numerous people during His earthly tenure who could quote Scripture or pretend that they knew and loved Him. But His reaction to them was always the same: "Show me the fruit."

Revolutionaries are Christ-followers who refuse to make excuses for their failings; instead, they address and overcome those inadequacies. Jesus did not die on the cross to fill church auditoriums, to enable magnificent church campuses to be funded, or to motivate people to implement innovative programs. He died because He loves you and me, He wants an everlasting relationship with us, and He expects that connection to be so all-consuming that we become wholly transformed—Jesus clones, if you will indulge the expression.

Does something get in the way of your living like Jesus? Then figure out how to eliminate that obstruction.

Does life get so complicated that it's difficult for you to juggle everything and remain Christlike? Then simplify your life.

Are you unable to find words that describe how you believe God has called you to know, love, and serve Him? Then develop new ways to communicate to others how God is ministering to you and through you.

Is society dragging you in the opposite direction from where Jesus calls you? Then acknowledge that your life is part of a spiritual war between God and Satan, declare your side, and get on with it. Admit that you are better off "fighting the good fight" and suffering on earth for the cause of Christ than winning the world but losing your soul for eternity.

Get used to the fact that your life is lived in the context of warfare. Every breath you take is an act of war. To survive and thrive in the midst of the spiritual battle in which you live, seek a faith context and experience that will enhance your capacity to be Christlike. This mission demands single-minded commitment and a disregard for the criticisms of those who lack the same dedication to the cause of Christ. You answer to only one Commander in Chief, and only you will give an explanation for your choices. Do whatever you have to do to prove that you fear God, you love Him, and you serve Him—yes, that you live *only* for Him.

That is the commitment of a Revolutionary.

chapter four

➤ HOW IS THE LOCAL CHURCH DOING?

LET ME BE COMPLETELY up front about this: My goal is to help you be a Revolutionary. I have been so moved by the spiritual authenticity of the Revolutionaries I have encountered—and so disappointed by much of what I have seen and measured among Christians in the United States over the last twenty-plus years—that I want to understand and be part of this groundbreaking development. I sense that this is one place where God is operating in a big-time way these days—and I don't want to get left out. Nor do I want you to be on the sidelines merely watching as the parade passes by.

Whether you become a Revolutionary immersed in, minimally involved in, or completely disassociated from a local church is irrelevant to me (and, within boundaries, to God). What matters is not whom you associate with (i.e., a local church), but who you are. I have spent the last twenty-four years of my life studying and working with a wide variety of churches: large and small; theologically liberal and conservative; wealthy and impoverished; urban, suburban, and rural; Caucasian and nonwhite; Protestant and Catholic;

located in the North, South, East, and West. I have spent countless hours reflecting on my experiences and observations related to those congregations and thousands of hours poring over statistical measures of what is happening in churches and in the spiritual lives of Americans. And, most importantly, I have studied God's Word regarding the Church.

After all this effort I must confess that I believe the French mathematician-philosopher Blaise Pascal was correct when he stated that all human beings have a God-shaped hole within them that they naturally attempt to fill, and that only a genuine relationship with the living God is capable of satisfying that emptiness. The reason is simple: Every human being was created by God primarily to know Him, love Him, and serve Him. All other activity is superfluous.

But that being the case raises some tough questions. One of them is simple: if the local church is God's answer to our spiritual needs, then why are most churched Christians so spiritually immature and desperate?

THE STATE OF CHURCHED CHRISTIANS

If the local church were the answer to our deep spiritual need, we would see two things. First, people who were most heavily involved in a Christian congregation would be more spiritually developed than others. Second, churched Christians would increasingly reflect the principles and characteristics Scripture tells us are the marks of Jesus' true disciples.

One of the greatest frustrations of my life has been the disconnection between what our research consistently shows about churched Christians and what the Bible calls us to be. Granted, we are sinful creatures and will never achieve perfection on this planet; only when we are reunited with God in heaven will we experience a fully restored state. However, if the local church is comprised of people who have been transformed by the grace of God through their redemption in Christ and the presence of the Holy Spirit, then their lives should be noticeably and compellingly different from the norm.

So let's take a look at the condition of the 77 million American adults who are churched, born-again Christians: people who have confessed their sins, asked God for forgiveness, accepted Jesus Christ as their Savior, are confident of their salvation solely because of the grace extended to them by God, and regularly participate in the life of a Christian congregation. Earlier we explored the seven passions of the first Christians; let's see if the same kind of transformation is evident in the lives of contemporary Christians.

Regarding Worship . . .
> The biweekly attendance at worship services is, by believers' own admission, generally the only time they worship God.
> Eight out of every ten believers do not feel they have entered into the presence of God, or experienced a connection with Him, during the worship service.
> Half of all believers say they do not feel they have

entered into the presence of God or experienced a genuine connection with Him during the past year.

> Only one out of every four churched believers says that when they worship God, they expect Him to be the primary beneficiary of their worship. (Most people say they expect to get the most from the experience.)

Regarding Faith-Based Conversations . . .

> The typical churched believer will die without leading a single person to a lifesaving knowledge of and relationship with Jesus Christ.

> At any given time, a majority of believers do not have a specific person in mind for whom they are praying in the hope that the person will be saved.

> Most churched Christians believe that since they are not gifted in evangelism, such outreach is not a significant responsibility of theirs.

Regarding Intentional Spiritual Growth . . .

> Only 9 percent of all born-again adults have a biblical worldview—meaning that less than one out of every ten Christians age eighteen or older believes that absolute moral truth exists, believes that such truth is contained in the Bible, and possesses a handful of core beliefs that reflect such truth. Those beliefs include a certainty that the Bible is accurate in its teachings; Jesus lived a sinless life on earth; Satan is real, not symbolic; all believers are responsible for sharing their faith in Christ with others; the only means to salvation is through God's grace; and

God is the all-knowing and all-powerful creator of the universe who still rules it today. The other 91 percent of born-again adults possess a patchwork of theological views and rarely rely upon those perspectives to inform their daily decisions.

> Although the typical believer contends that the Bible is accurate in what it teaches, he or she spends less time reading the Bible in a year than watching television, listening to music, reading other books and publications, or conversing about personal hobbies and leisure interests.

> When asked what constitutes success in life, few believers define *success* in spiritual terms. Most describe outcomes related to professional achievement, family solidarity, physical accomplishments, or resource acquisition.

> When given the opportunity to state how they want to be known by others, fewer than one out of ten believers mentioned descriptions that reflect their relationship with God.

Regarding Resource Investment . . .

> Churched Christians give away an average of about 3 percent of their income in a typical year—and feel pleased at their "sacrificial" generosity.

> Fewer than one out of every ten churched Christians donates at least 10 percent of their income to churches and other nonprofit organizations. (More than one-third claim to do so.)

> When asked to explain their understanding of biblical

stewardship, less than one out of every twenty includes resources such as time, relationships, ideas, or skills in their assessment.

> Most believers are unable to identify anything specific they have ever donated money to that they would describe as producing life-changing outcomes.

Regarding Servanthood . . .

> In a typical week, only one out of every four believers will allocate some time to serving other people. Most of that time is dedicated to volunteering in church programs that serve congregants; little effort is invested in serving needy people outside the congregation.

> Most churched Christians admit to having seen homeless or hurting people in their community or travels during the past year; a very small percentage says they interacted with any of those disadvantaged individuals.

> The typical believer would rather give money to an organization to allow it to do good deeds in society than personally assist in alleviating the needs of disadvantaged people.

Regarding Spiritual Friendships . . .

> Fewer than one out of every six churched believers has a relationship with another believer through which spiritual accountability is provided.

> The most significant influence on the choices of churched believers is neither teachings from the pulpit nor advice gleaned from fellow congregants; it is

messages absorbed from the media, the law, and family members.

Regarding Family Faith . . .

- A large majority of churched believers rely upon their church, rather than their family, to train their children to become spiritually mature.
- In an average month, fewer than one out of every ten churched families worships together outside of a church service; just as few pray together, other than at mealtimes; and the same minimal numbers study the Bible together at home or work together to address the needs of disadvantaged people in their community.
- The likelihood of a married couple who are born-again churchgoers getting divorced is the same as couples who are not disciples of Jesus.
- Apart from church-based programs, the typical Christian family spends less than three hours per month in endeavors designed to jointly develop or apply their faith.
- Most Christian parents do not believe they are doing a good job at facilitating the spiritual development of their children.

THE SOURCE OF HOPE

The point of this exercise is not to bash the local church. Christian churches have an incredible two-thousand-year legacy of pursuing God and faithfully doing His work. An extraordinary repository of life-changing results emanates from the work of churches. It is horrifying to imagine what the world would be like if the local church had not been present to represent Jesus in manifold ways. It is not a perfect group of people or a perfect institution; it is populated by sinners—like you and me—whom God dearly loves, despite our debased nature. And despite its faults and flaws, a spiritually healthy local church will always have a valid and valuable role within God's Kingdom on earth.

The point here is simply to recognize that if we place all our hope in the local church, it is a misplaced hope. Many well-intentioned pastors promote this perspective by proclaiming, "The local church is the hope of the world." Like most advertising slogans, this notion is emotionally appealing. The trouble is, the sentiment is not biblical. *Jesus, and Jesus alone, is the hope of the world.* The local church is one mechanism that can be instrumental in bringing us closer to Him and helping us to be more like Him. But, as the research data clearly show, churches are not doing the job. If the local church is the hope of the world, then the world has no hope.

THE LOCAL CHURCH

There is nothing inherently wrong with being involved in a local church. But realize that being part of a group that calls itself a "church" does not make you saved, holy, righteous, or godly any more than being in Yankee Stadium makes you a professional baseball player. Participating in church-based activities does not necessarily draw you closer to God or prepare you for a life that satisfies Him or enhances your existence. Being a member of a congregation does not make you spiritually righteous any more than being a member of the Democratic Party makes you a liberal wing nut.

Being in a right relationship with God and His people is what matters. Scripture teaches us that devoting your life to loving God with all your heart, mind, strength, and soul is what honors Him. Being part of a local church may facilitate that. Or it might not.

Sadly, many people will label this view "blasphemy." However, you should realize that *the Bible neither describes nor promotes the local church as we know it today.* Many centuries ago religious leaders created the prevalent form of "church" that is so widespread in our society to help people be better followers of Christ. But the local church many have come to cherish—the services, offices, programs, buildings, ceremonies—is neither biblical nor unbiblical. It is abiblical—that is, such an organization is not addressed in the Bible.

In fact, if you scour the Bible passages included at the beginning of Chapter 3, you will find no allusions to or descriptions of a specific type of religious organization or spiritual form. The Bible does not rigidly define the corporate practices, rituals, or structures that must be embraced in order to have a proper church. It does, however, offer direction regarding the importance and integration of fundamental spiritual disciplines into one's life. Sometimes we forget that the current forms of religious practice and community were developed hundreds of years ago, long after the Bible was written, in an attempt to help believers live more fulfilling Christian lives. We should keep in mind that what we call "church" is just one interpretation of how to develop and live a faith-centered life. We made it up. It may be healthy or helpful, but it is not sacrosanct.

The Revolution is not about eliminating, dismissing, or disparaging the local church. It is about building relationships, commitments, processes, and tools that enable us to be the God-lovers we were intended to be from the beginning of creation. Revolutionaries realize—sometimes very reluctantly—that the core issue isn't whether or not one is involved in a local church, but whether or not one is connected to the body of believers in the pursuit of godliness and worship. Consequently, the Revolution involves the remnant of believers who are obsessed with practicing the same seven passions that defined the early Church, in order to be agents of transformation in this world.

You see, it's not about *church*. It's about *the Church*—that is, the people who actively participate in the intentional advancement of God's Kingdom in partnership with the Holy Spirit and other believers.

THE REVOLUTIONARY RESPONSE

Our research indicates that Revolutionaries fill all points on the continuum of church involvement. Some are pastors or lay leaders in a church. Some are heavily involved in the activities of a church, even though they do not have a leadership position. Some Revolutionaries are more tangentially involved, irregularly attending but adding value when they do. Other Revolutionaries harbor no ill will toward churches but out of extreme frustration or disillusionment have developed alternative means of growing and serving that are distinct from local church efforts.

The Revolutionary mind-set is simple: Do whatever it takes to get closer to God and to help others to do the same. Obliterate any obstacle that prevents you from honoring God with every breath you take. Be such an outstanding example of the Christian faith that no one will question your heart or lifestyle—except those who see institutional survival as equally or more important than the alleged influence of the institution they defend.

Or, put more succinctly, the Revolution is about recognizing that we are not called to *go* to church. We are called to *be* the Church.

chapter five

> SPIRITUAL TRANSITIONS IN THE MAKING

CHANGE IS A NATURAL, positive, and irreplaceable part of growth. Leaders often remind us that what got us where we are is not the same stuff that will get us where we want to go, so we must change. Psychologists remind us that repeating the same behaviors merely generates the same outcomes, and therefore precludes rather than produces positive change. In other words, to grow, we must purposefully alter our routines and approaches. And the Bible is equally clear in telling us that God did not send Jesus to die so we might be comfortable and complacent, but so we might die to self, pick up our cross, and follow the way of the Master.

The spiritual Revolution that is gathering momentum and influence in America provides evidence of sweeping changes that are taking place today. Some of the most important trends that are reshaping our society relate to the shift in worldview, lifestyle, and expectations that characterize our two youngest generations: the Baby Busters and the Mosaics. In fact, I believe seven particular trends are leading to the New Church that will facilitate the moral and spiritual revolution that millions of us have been praying for over the past several decades.

What are those seven trends?

Trend #1: The Changing of the Guard

The two generations that contain people in their forties, fifties, sixties, and seventies—the Baby Boomers and the Builders—are slowly and painstakingly losing their grip on power in society. It is the two younger generations of Americans—the Baby Busters and the Mosaics—who inject energy into the economy, social institutions, and even the Church because they understand and embrace constant change and innovation. Over the coming decade, increasing numbers of these younger adults will ascend to positions of power and influence.

As a result of the passing of the torch, Busters (those born from 1965 through 1983) and Mosaics (born from 1984 to 2002) are altering the ways in which people relate to each other, the types of outcomes deemed desirable, the procedures used to achieve meaningful results, the values and beliefs that underlie critical decisions, and the role of technology in our lives. These same transitions are radically affecting how people perceive and practice their faith.

Trend #2: The Rise of a New View of Life

Philosophically, America is now a "postmodern" society. Postmodernism claims there are no moral absolutes—that is, truth is whatever you believe it to be. That kind of thinking suggests that good citizenship requires tolerance of all points of view and behavioral preferences. The postmodern philosophy also proclaims that the most important element in life is your relationships; that the processes you engage in are more significant than the product of those procedures, which is a "means justify the ends" perspective; and that the most appropriate route to influence is through dialogue, not monologue or the imposition of one's beliefs or approaches upon others.

This shift into a live-and-let-live philosophy affects every dimension of our lives, including the ways in which we understand and practice Christianity. Obviously, some of the central elements of this spreading philosophy—such as its rejection of absolute moral truth—are at odds with being a disciple of Jesus Christ. Other core principles, such as the emphasis on relationships, are consistent with the teachings of the Lord. The threat to the Church lies in the fact that surprisingly few Americans are sufficiently reflective about the implications of this shift to critically assess its pros and cons—and to know when it is important to take a stand against the encroachment of unbiblical principles.

Trend #3: Dismissing the Irrelevant

One of the legacies of the Baby Boomer generation is the unwillingness to put up with irrelevance. Boomers are infamous for demanding excellence in everything they encounter. Entities that fail to live up to the standards of our largest and richest generation are quickly dismissed.

The post-Boomer crowd has mutated that perspective. Excellence is less meaningful to them because it sometimes reflects the slickness of exploitation and manipulation. The pet peeve of the younger generations is irrelevance: they quickly abandon anything that is not wholly germane to their personal passions. They have significantly altered expectations and lifestyles through their demand that things foster shared experience and be "real," adventuresome, and memorable. They have little patience for anything based on tradition, customs, ease, or social acceptability. If they do not immediately sense the relevance of something, they dismiss it out of hand and move on to the next alternative. Remember, in a culture where the individual is king and there are no absolute moral truths, exercising choice without limitations is a cherished right.

Trend #4: The Impact of Technology

Few of our daily experiences have remained outside the influence of the technologies introduced in the past twenty years. Communications, medicine, information dissemination and storage, education, farming, athletics, music and art—you name it and the chances are high that it has been seriously affected by technology in recent years. And that includes the faith dimension, too.

Among the most overt effects on church life have been applications such as the widespread embrace of large-screen projection systems for worship and teaching events; the use of video technology for multisite ministry; satellite delivery of ministry training; the ubiquity of religious conversation in the media (including the Internet); congregations' reliance on Web sites for disseminating ministry information; the use of computers, the Internet, and e-mail for gathering facts that are woven into religious teaching; the enhanced visual design evident in church publications and presentations; and the superior musical experiences provided through the use of downloadable files and performances using "smart" instruments.

The implications of this advanced technology in relation to ministry include the reshaping of the marketplace, the reorientation of community into new forms and relationships, the expectation of finding ministry resources that respond directly to both felt and real needs, a heightened awareness of global faith conditions and opportunities, and the desire to be part of a worldwide Church with localized applications.

Trend #5: Genuine Relationships

Busters and Mosaics place a much higher premium on genuine personal relationships than do their predecessors. They are not necessarily more adept at this process. But they certainly pursue meaningful relationships rather than passing acquaintances, and they are more likely to invest themselves in the messiness of other people's issues than to pass along superficial advice. They devote a greater share of their time each day to keeping up those bonds. They are, in the vernacular, "people people."

As Busters and Mosaics wield their increasing influence in the development of media content, institutional behavioral patterns, the reshaping of societal customs, and accepted notions regarding relational activity, we are becoming a society increasingly focused on personal authenticity rather than excellence in performance. As the years go by, the balance of excellence and authenticity will gradually shift to the latter. In ministry and other areas, we will emphasize personal stories and experience instead of principles and commands. We will show a growing appreciation for leaders who operate within a team context rather than those who exhibit charisma and dynamism as captivating solo practitioners. Organizations that demonstrate inclusiveness will grab our allegiance over those that are perceived to be narrow or judgmental.

Trend #6: Participation in Reality
Americans are known for being hands-on, entrepreneurial people. With the proliferation of technology, the rise of women in positions of marketplace leadership, and the educational emphasis upon the practical rather than the conceptual, people expect to be active and creative participants in developing the reality of their experience. Fewer and fewer people are willing to sit back and endure what the world throws at them; rather, they are seeking the means to exert greater control over their lives. As time goes on, people are paying more attention to the outcomes their efforts generate and are constantly refining their activity to generate more personally satisfying results.

The same mind-set is affecting the ministry context. There is more enthusiasm for creating personal dialogue with non-Christian friends than for bringing them to a big evangelistic event. The popularity of small groups has grown consistently as people experience the benefits of a shared experience in which their contribution matters. Short-term missions activity has exploded as growing numbers of Christians want to be part of a ministry solution rather than merely fund it. Watch how the next few years will usher in innovative expressions of this hands-on approach to being a Christian in a non-Christian world.

Trend #7: Finding True Meaning

Every generation wades through the murky waters of life's meaning. The discovery process is never easy, and the answers are often a long time coming. The eternal struggle to find meaning in life—which cannot occur without recognizing how God has designed us and how to apply that design to the context in which we live—is in full force today. Despite all the advances in technology and communications, our society's complexity and fragmentation have only served to heighten the struggle to make sense of our place in the world.

One of the most startling signs of growth, though, is Americans' accelerated openness to understanding themselves through two components that have been largely ignored for many decades: sacrifice and surrender. Granted, this commitment or pattern is not widespread at this moment, but we are seeing growing numbers of people who are considering sacrifice and surrender as the possible missing links to their maturation and fulfillment.

THE NEW SPIRITUAL LANDSCAPE

Whether or not you currently understand the implications of these trends, two things are true. First, you don't have to like the outcomes of things you cannot change, but you do have to deal with them. Second, the more you can anticipate some of the transitions resulting from these trends, the greater will be your ability to help shape the world in ways that are likely to honor God and advance your spiritual maturity. This will impact your own life and the lives of others with whom you interact.

What outcomes are likely in the spiritual landscape of the country as a result of these seven trends?

Perhaps the most significant relates to how increasing numbers of people will be most likely to experience and express their faith in the coming years. A radical transformation is in progress related to the means through which people's faith is made real.

As we entered the twenty-first century, the local church was the focus of most people's spiritual lives. About 70 percent of all Americans relied upon some local congregation to be their dominant source of spiritual input and output. A few individuals—roughly 5 percent of the population—were engaged in a faith journey that revolved around some alternative type of faith community. (We'll look at these in more detail later in the book.) A similarly small percentage of people identified their family as their primary faith pod. A larger, but still minority, group of Americans (an estimated 20 percent) turned to various cultural sources—the media, the arts, or other institutions—as the outlets designated to satisfy their faith needs.

The seven cultural trends described earlier, however, have unleashed a massive shift in emphasis. As I have tracked people's inclinations through our national research studies, I have concluded that by the year 2025, the spiritual profile of the nation will be dramatically different. Specifically, I expect that only about one-third of the population will rely upon a local congregation as the primary or exclusive means for experiencing and expressing their faith; one-third will do so through alternative forms of a faith-based community; and one-third will realize their faith through the media, the arts, and other cultural institutions. Unfortunately, as far as we can determine, the family will remain a mere blip on the radar screen when it comes to serving as the conduit for faith experience and expression, remaining central to perhaps 5 percent of the population.

How Americans Experience and Express Their Faith

Primary means of spiritual experience and expression

	Local Church	Alternative Faith-Based Community	Family	Media, Arts, Culture
2000	70%	5%	5%	20%
2025	30-35%	30-35%	5%	30-35%

You may read this and feel a sense of loss or dread—or you may celebrate the development of new ways people can grow to full maturity in their faith. The relatively compromised and complacent state of faith in the nation today suggests that any new means through which people—especially younger people—can make their faith come alive and become more center stage in their lives, without conflicting with scriptural imperatives, will represent a welcome breath of fresh air in the stagnant spiritual landscape of our country.

And do not forget the first of the two admonitions provided at the start of this section: You don't have to like this transition, but you must deal with it. You can approach it with a defensive, negative attitude, or you can deal with it in the hope of learning and experiencing great breakthroughs in your life. That choice is yours.

chapter six

➤ GOD IS ACTIVE TODAY

CULTURAL ICONS are often remembered for a single moment or product that defined their career. The renowned German philosopher Friedrich Nietzsche is one of those one-note examples. He is widely known today for popularizing the notion that "God is dead."

I'd hate to have Nietzsche's legacy. Why? Because he is wrong. How do I know? Because of the numerous individuals we have interviewed and studied in the course of our research whose lives have been radically transformed by a real and lasting encounter with the living God. There is nothing more affirming than knowing that God is active in the lives of those who seek His touch, and nothing more exciting than seeing the passion and enthusiasm of those people for the God who has revealed Himself in such personal and restorative ways.

A WORD ABOUT *TRANSFORMATION*

One of my pet peeves is that we sometimes use a word so indiscriminately that it ceases to have any true meaning. For example, in the 2004 presidential election, everyone who attended a theologically conservative church was deemed an "evangelical." More generally, everyone who attends a Protestant or Catholic church is labeled a "Christian." Everyone participating in a cell group or small group is said to have spiritual "accountability."

You might have a different understanding of the term *transformation* than I do. It's crucial to our discussion, since the Revolution is so centered on the idea that each of us is called to be continually transformed through the renewing and reshaping power of the Holy Spirit. Let me explain the intended meaning of the term.

Spiritual transformation is any significant and lasting transition in your life wherein you switch from one substantial perspective or practice to something wholly different that genuinely alters you at a very basic level.

Switching from a Methodist church to a Presbyterian church is not transformational; determining to live in accordance with a biblical worldview is.

Attending a Sunday school class after years of absence is not transformation; identifying one's giftedness, grasping the call to use those gifts for Kingdom outcomes, and initiating a lifestyle of service to others is.

Agreeing to lead a small group every week is a wonderful choice, but it is usually not transformational. Seeing the beauty of the lake you drive by on the way to work every day; the inherent preciousness of the children hanging out at the playground; and the blessing of having a warm, dry, comfortable house in which to live, as examples of the infinite reasons to constantly worship God every hour of every day—and then doing so—is truly transformational.

Transformation, as I am using it, is a significant spiritual breakthrough in which you seize a new perspective or practice related to the seven passions; consequently, you are never the same again. The transformation redefines who you are at a fundamental spiritual level, and your lifestyle is realigned according to that part of your being that was finally awakened to the things of God.

Our research revealed that God is, indeed, busy transforming people's lives. But it also uncovered some shocking truths about *how* God is bringing about such transformation in our society.

DISCOVERING SPIRITUAL MINI-MOVEMENTS

My original assumption as we set out to profile the hallmarks of contemporary spiritual transformation was that most of the life change we found would be related to the ministry of the local church. We spent several years searching for evidence that God was at work changing lives through churches and discovering how that process worked. While we certainly found some wonderful examples, I was stunned—and deeply disappointed—at how relatively rare such instances were.

But our conversations with churchgoing people and congregational leaders led us to the primary source of such transformation: ministries operating outside of the local church. These were not all "parachurch" ministries, per se, but they were God-centered endeavors taking place outside of a congregational connection. As I began encountering more and more of these situations, I realized that God is very much alive and well, busy transforming lives through what we have been calling "spiritual mini-movements."

As time went on, it became clear that God is affecting lives through many of these mini-movements, reaching literally millions of people. You are probably connected to some of them, or to people involved in them, without realizing their significance. Some of these mini-movements include homeschooling, "simple church" fellowships (i.e., house churches), biblical worldview groups, various marketplace ministries, several spiritual disciplines networks, the Christian creative arts guilds, and others.

Most of the religious analysts I confer with are only vaguely aware of these groups—and completely unaware of their spiritual significance within the Church today. There are three major reasons why the mini-movements have flown below the radar screen. First, their numbers are relatively small. Most of the dozen mini-movements that we have studied most closely have fewer than three million adherents. In a nation of about 300 million people, that is too miniscule to be perceived as significant and too dispersed to draw attention.

Second, in most cases, the mini-movements themselves are disorganized and even disunited. While God is at work affecting the lives of the individuals involved, the group with which the transformed individual is associated tends to be poorly structured, inadequately led, and lacking in any larger, strategic framework or purpose. In fact, this is one of the more powerful arguments that the life changes occurring are God-driven and not man-made: the mini-movements themselves are struggling to achieve health!

Third, there is a pervasive mind-set among many journalists, scholars, and religious leaders that all legitimate spiritual activity must flow through a local church. Even large parachurch ministries that communicate with tens of millions of people, raise hundreds of millions of dollars, and impact lives all over the world are cast as second fiddle to the local church. It is almost as if their ministry efforts are deemed subpar simply because they did not originate from a congregational context.

Nevertheless, the emergence of these mini-movements reminded me that God is no respecter of persons—or the false boundaries they create to control their environment. Whether religious leaders deem it appropriate or not, God is facilitating incredible transformation in the minds and hearts of millions of people involved with the mini-movements. Why? Perhaps because these people have made the faith orientation of the mini-movement the pivot point of their existence. They want more of God in their lives, so they invest themselves in the workings of the mini-movement, focusing on the distinctive emphasis of the group, whether it is all-out worship, heartfelt prayer, developing a Christian mind, or whatever the driving motivation of the group may be. It is that single-mindedness of intent and the intensity of their focus on God that enables the Lord to build them into Revolutionaries.

THE LOCAL CHURCH RESPONDS

A disturbing discovery from our research, though, was the reaction of local churches to how God was touching the lives of people in the mini-movements. More often than not, impacted individuals would return to their local churches and share their faith adventure with a church leader. Usually, their desire was to work with their leaders to find ways to incorporate the magnificent work of God that they had personally experienced into the ministry of the church. Even though God had changed them through mechanisms based outside the efforts of the local churches, most of these people demonstrated loyalty to their congregations, seeking to integrate their experience into the overall ministry of their church.

However, in the majority of cases, the leaders of the local church suggested that the transformed believers simply continue to do whatever it was they were doing, and not try to introduce foreign elements into the church's agenda. In other words, let the church carry out its existing slate of events and programs without attempting to alter a stable and well-planned ministry simply because one or several congregants had discovered distinctive ways of connecting with and being shaped by God.

To their credit, most of the transformed people we have interviewed reflected the attitude of Peter and John, who said to the leaders who rebuked them, "We cannot stop telling about everything we have seen and heard" (Acts 4:20). Deeply moved by the experiences brought about through their involvement in the mini-movement, they continued to seek growth opportunities through it while staying connected to other ministries, fellow believers, and their church.

The result has been the gradual expansion of the reach and impact of those mini-movements. Every year, millions of people are being radically affected by the presence and power of God that is manifested through those low-profile ministries. While no particular ministry or mini-movement has emerged to become the focal point of spiritual growth in the United States, the impact of these groups is massive, albeit virtually invisible. The cumulative effect is nothing short of the redefinition of the nature and face of ministry in our world.

THE SECRET OF TRANSFORMATION

How is it that these mini-movements have fostered impressive life changes when many local churches have failed to produce similar outcomes—often with the same people? My research among these transformed individuals indicates at least five common conditions within these streams of ministry that produce such spectacular change.

First, the mini-movements are generally working with people who are predisposed to focusing on their faith in God. In other words, these people are Revolutionaries because they have made a decision to prioritize their faith. Once they have made that decision, it simply becomes a matter of which connections will most readily foster transformation.

Second, the mini-movement emerges as a prime candidate for engendering such growth because it becomes an individual's primary source of relationships. The conversations and experiences shared by the people in the movement become a kind of closed circle that energizes itself to the point of multiplied returns on the investment. The level of accountability and the heightened focus on spiritual development generate very positive outcomes.

Third, the intimacy experienced within the mini-movement facilitates a sense of exhilaration over the transformation. That emanates from a fourth characteristic of the mini-movements: clear group goals. Since these entities exist to encourage positive spiritual growth, their planned activities center on such results. When those results are evident, word travels fast, and there is a general feeling of joy.

A fifth observation is that each of the mini-movements establishes its place in a person's life through a very narrow focus—prayer, worship, worldview, musical expression, or whatever. However, that focus typically serves primarily as an entryway into the mind and heart of the individual. Often, once the person becomes immersed in the activity of the mini-movement, he or she is presented with a variety of spiritual challenges and opportunities that get blended into transformational activities.

Again, one artifact of the mini-movement phenomenon has been that millions of people who are growing as Christians and passionate about their faith have come to recognize that the local church is not—and need not be—the epicenter of their spiritual adventure. This is a mind-boggling realization for many since it conflicts with the teaching they have received, sometimes since their infancy. But many report that it has been a freeing insight. It has enabled them to mature in unique ways that may not have happened had they closed themselves off to the possibility of God meeting them in other ways or places.

But make no mistake about it: God is still active in the lives of those people who are wholeheartedly devoted to and searching for Him—no matter what door they enter on their journey to Christlikeness.

chapter seven

> A NEW WAY OF DOING CHURCH

A CENTURY AGO, carmaker Henry Ford professed his willingness to give people choice in their selection of color for his cars. "People can have a Model T in any color they want—as long as it's black." That's pretty similar to the view of many Americans regarding how people should pursue spiritual growth—through any means they want, as long as it is connected to the efforts of a local church.

As previously noted, however, the Revolution is changing the way in which people anchor their faith pursuits. For some Revolutionaries, their congregational experience is the linchpin of their faith journey. For many others, a local church plays a minor role in their journey. For millions of others, the local church is nowhere to be found on their agenda. Yet a majority of Revolutionaries are involved in some form of "church."

If this sounds like one of those brain-teasing Mensa puzzles, it's not. The church connection has to do with the new models of "church" that are being conceived, developed, explored, and embraced by millions of Americans, including many Revolutionaries. The congregational model, which is the dominant form of the "church" experience today, is rapidly being joined—and, for millions of Revolutionaries, replaced—by various alternatives.

REASONS FOR THE SHIFT

The congregational model of the church—a definable group of people who regularly meet at the same place to engage in religious routines and programs under the guidance of a paid pastor who provides doctrinal teaching and organizational direction—has been the dominant force in people's spiritual lives for hundreds of years. So why is it so rapidly losing ground at this moment in history?

Perhaps the major reasons are people's insistence on choices and their desire to have customized experiences. The issue of choice is remaking many facets of modern experience. Whether you examine the changes in broadcasting, clothing, music, investing, or automobiles, producers of such consumables realize that Americans want control over their lives. The result has been the "niching" of America—creating highly refined categories that serve smaller numbers of people, but can command greater loyalty (and profits). During the past three decades, even the local church has undergone such a niching process, with the advent of churches designed for different generations, those offering divergent styles of worship music, congregations that emphasize ministries of interest to specialized populations, and so forth.

The church landscape now offers these boutique churches alongside the something-for-everybody megachurches. In the religious marketplace, the churches that have suffered most are those who stuck with the one-size-fits-all approach, typically proving that one-size-fits-nobody. Whether the niche-orientation of a church was designed to provide yet another alternative to choose from, to satisfy an underserved market (i.e., create a customized experience), or to address previously unmet or misunderstood needs (i.e., provide relevance), new models hit a hot button in a need-meeting culture.

But the motivations for seeking new models do not stop there. Other drivers behind the move to new models include the preference for practical faith experiences, rather than generic, conceptual faith; a quest for spiritual depth and breadth, rather than settling for one dimension or the other; a penchant for novelty and creativity, rather than predictability in religious experiences; and the need for time-shifting, rather than inflexible scheduling of religious events.

One outcome of the multifaceted push for new spiritual models has been the rise of unique, highly personalized church experiences. Few people now have the same faith development patterns and resources that comprise their journey. Two decades ago, typical Christians went to Sunday school at nine o'clock Sunday morning, then flowed into the worship service at eleven. They might have participated in a Bible study group or maybe a family service on Wednesday evening at seven. And many believers prayed before meals and at the beginning or end of their day, and read the Bible a couple of mornings before settling into their daytime routine.

Now it's virtually impossible to craft a "typical" spiritual pattern, especially among people under the age of forty. Growing numbers of young adults, teenagers, and even adolescents are piecing together spiritual elements they deem worthwhile, constituting millions of personalized "church" models. The proliferation of new elements available through the Internet, television, radio, diversified social networks, community action cooperatives, and via live arts environments is ensuring that future models of "church" will be almost impossible to categorize or market.

TWO VARIATIONS ON A THEME

One way of understanding the impact of the Revolution on the local church is to see how it is introducing a universe of faith-based models into the mix. Some of these are "macro-models"—that is, all-inclusive faith communities that address the complete array of passions that lead a person to a Christlike life. Other expressions are "micro-models"—narrowly focused assemblies that commit to genuine growth in relation to one of the seven spiritual passions in particular.

There are four macro-models of church experience resident in the nation today. The dominant force is the *congregational form of the local church. House churches*—some call them "simple church" fellowships—are yet another holistic model. These are small aggregations of people who meet in someone's home on a regular basis to fulfill all the functions of a traditional congregation, especially elements such as worship, teaching, fellowship, and stewardship. (Note: these are not the same as the widespread small groups, cell groups, and home fellowships that are spawned by local churches to supplement what occurs on the local church campus.) The *family faith experience* is a third holistic model, in which the family becomes the primary spiritual unit and pursues faith matters together, with parents and their children (and, often, members of the extended family) becoming a close-knit faith community. The fourth holistic model is the *cyberchurch*. This refers to the range of spiritual experiences delivered through the Internet.

It is worth noting that the two fastest-growing macro-models of church are the house church and cyberchurch formations.

But it is the micro-models that are growing the fastest of all. These might be considered the *distributed* models of faith. These models promote growth in a specific aspect of the seven passions, expecting that the energy released through that focus will motivate the believer to incorporate growth in the other areas of passion as well.

One of the best examples of micro-models is the popularity of independent worship events that occur throughout the nation. Not associated with a specific church or denomination, these gatherings feature one or more "worship gypsies"—individuals like Chris Tomlin, David Crowder, Matt Redman, Tim Hughes, and dozens of regional favorites—who constantly travel to gatherings of believers, playing extended sets of worship music for audiences who had no prior connection to each other. The events are designed to help people connect with God through an intense worship experience. Often, the event leads those who participated to not only upgrade their worship quotient but also get more serious about other aspects of their spiritual life. The event makes no attempt to build a congregation or enduring local ministry of any type. The effort is geared toward getting people to worship God and grow from that foundation.

Other distributed models include marketplace fellowships, coaching communities, and narrowcast Internet-based faith groups, as well as the prolific number of parachurch ministries that are generally unidimensional in their focus. A hallmark of such distributed models is that they are not simply one-time events but are part of a larger ministry effort designed to supplement the person's incremental spiritual growth.

FUTURE MODELS

Will there be a macro-model, similar in magnitude to the congregational format of the local church, to replace that dominant but declining model? It does not seem likely. In fact, some extensions of the congregational model, such as the "emergent" or "postmodern" congregations, really are not new models but simply minor refinements of the reigning model. Ultimately, we expect to see believers choosing from a proliferation of options, weaving together a set of favored alternatives into a unique tapestry that constitutes the personal "church" of the individual.

While this patchwork of spiritual experiences and expressions will produce a seemingly incoherent and indecipherable religious landscape, it will also render people's spiritual lives more exciting because they'll be able to respond to immediate needs and possibilities. The fragmented nature of the new approach to spirituality, often lamented by analysts as an unfortunate consequence of our disjointed culture and spiritually illiterate population, will become the advantage that facilitates a deeper commitment to spiritual focus by millions of young people.

As for the Revolution, it is composed of millions of people who have already embraced the freedom and excitement introduced through new macro- and micro-models. The central message of the Revolution rings out from these experiences: Revolutionaries will respond to the presence and principles of God whenever and wherever possible, without regard to historical or societal inhibitions. The standard that concerns Revolutionaries is simple: does the mechanism provide a way of advancing my faith, without compromising Scripture or any of the passions of a true believer?

chapter eight

> JESUS THE REVOLUTIONARY

EARLIER WE NOTED that Webster defined a revolutionary as someone committed to the thorough replacement of an established system of government in the hope of seeing radical change in society and social structures.

Various historians have argued that Jesus Christ was the most significant person in history, having the deepest and broadest influence of any person ever. Few profiles of world-changers leave Him out of the mix. Whether He gets the top ranking or not, the fact that people around the world continue to recognize His lasting impact on humanity some two millennia after His departure from earth is evidence of a revolutionary life.

We also noted that Jesus Christ is the focal point of the life of every Christian Revolutionary today. It is His call to revolutionary living that beckons us and guides us on this path.

His effect on the world is undeniable. You and I would not be interacting on these matters if it had not been for His life. But what made Jesus a Revolutionary? Since we are commanded to be imitators of Christ, what should we learn from His example?

CHRIST'S PERSPECTIVE

Two crucial insights into the revolutionary lifestyle can be gleaned from how Jesus behaved on earth.

The first relates to the objective of replacing an established system of government. We know that Jesus was not a political reformer in the sense of seeking position or power in the public arena. But He did want to reform government—*self-government*. His message was clear: you cannot rely upon public policies and the enforcement of laws to shape your character and lifestyle. It is not your title, fame, fortune, or network that gives you lasting influence; that comes from who you are, in light of your character, your values, and your core beliefs. It is those components that drive the decisions and activities in your life.

So if you are a Revolutionary, it is because you have sensed and responded to God's calling to be such an imitator of Christ. It is not a church's responsibility to make you into this mold. It is not society's job to push you in this direction. You are responsible for who you are. The choice to become a Revolutionary—and it is a choice—is a covenant you make with God alone. The commands and admonitions provided by Jesus to all who would listen were designed to facilitate self-governance that makes each disciple a revolution in progress.

The second insight relates to how an appropriately self-governed follower of Jesus is expected to live. In John 17,

Jesus spoke to His followers regarding their responsibility, giving birth to the widely known but inadequately invoked calling to "be in, but not of, this world." In other words, through consistent devotion to biblical principles manifested in a noticeably different mind-set and lifestyle, the disciple is called to *influence the world* rather than to be influenced by it.

In a similar manner, then, you and I are called to be Revolutionaries by conforming to the will of God and letting that affect every life and decision within our reach. We are not Revolutionaries because we join a community of like minded people, although such ties are integral to our personal development and our spiritual identity. We become Revolutionaries through our absolute commitment to think and behave like Jesus in order to show our love for God, and to love other people through our positive influence on their lives.

What does a Revolutionary's life look like? Jesus showed us that our strategy is evident through our priorities. His example teaches that the weapons we use are our demeanor, character, and the presence of the Holy Spirit of God working through us. And His words instruct us that the mark of success is the identity and the commitment we bring to the role.

JESUS' FOLLOW-THROUGH

No person ever practiced what he preached better than Jesus did. If His assignment for us is to be Revolutionaries, we have an intimate knowledge of what that means largely through His earthly example. He was relentlessly self-disciplined. The consistency of His words and behavior transformed every place and every person He encountered.

I encourage you to take some time to read the Gospel accounts of Jesus' life with the intention of discerning the attributes and actions that gave Him this power to transform. Too often we write off His influence, protesting that He was, after all, God, and therefore His ways are beyond our grasp. But that's just an excuse we hide behind to avoid the challenge of Revolutionary living. His life is our model. A true Revolutionary accepts the challenge to be fully Christlike, as impossible as it may seem at the start of that quest. Remember, nobody starts out a champion; only those who are single-minded in their determination to reach lofty goals become unrivaled leaders.

As you study the Gospels for lessons and clues, notice that Jesus ignored customs, expectations, and even laws in order to be all that God intended. His focus shows us, in the flesh, what is possible and how to make the most of every opportunity provided by God. Let's take a brief look at His life, seen in the book of Matthew, to discover how you can transcend the moral and spiritual gravity of this world to enter a Revolutionary orbit.

His Identity

Jesus had the right to have a chip on His shoulder. But from the moment we meet Him, all we find is humility. Think about His choices and how He responded to various circumstances. He was baptized by someone whose very salvation was dependent upon being forgiven by Jesus. He refused to accept titles or even simple accolades. He did nothing to call attention to Himself; in fact, He generally shunned the spotlight and avoided situations that would bring notoriety and acclaim. He consistently exhorted people to demonstrate humility and to realize that their stature is determined by God, not by what they or others say.

Despite the human tendency to proclaim and prove one's independence, Jesus recognized and freely acknowledged His total dependence upon God. In both His public ministry and His private life, He lived as a servant seeking to be used by God the Father. His self-worth was not based on His own performance; it was based on how faithfully He did the will of God and operated in the power of the Spirit.

Unlike many people who assume power or influence, Jesus was never under the delusion that His service to humankind would produce universal applause and adulation. Aware that He was a warrior in the invisible spiritual battle, the Man from Galilee went to great lengths to preach to His colleagues and prepare them to embrace their inevitable social standing: targets for misunderstanding, hatred, discrimination, and persecution. The picture He painted for fellow Revolutionaries was appallingly unattractive—and it reflected His acute awareness of His place on earth.

One of the most intriguing insights into Jesus is His recognition that He was a person in process. He perceived the many trials and challenges He endured as means of demonstrating

His worthiness and shaping His character. As Jesus the divine Son, He was truly complete; but as Jesus the Deity made human, He underwent many of the same growth pains that we experience. Perhaps that refined sense of timing enabled Him to have greater patience with the daily battles He faced.

The most compelling aspect of His self-image, though, is that He understood His role to be a twofold mission: to love God and to love people. That perception is simple but not at all simplistic. As the embodiment of love, Jesus tangibly modeled various facets of love—compassionate love, tough love, enduring love, forgiving love—as well as the dramatic impact authentic love has on the world.

Our self-image creates the infrastructure through which we respond to the world. What are the lessons for you and me in how Jesus, the Savior of the world, saw Himself?

His Priorities in Life

You devote yourself to doing what you believe is the highest priority in life. Sometimes you may protest that you're a victim of circumstances or others' expectations, but your choices reflect what you believe to be most important.

Jesus clarified His priorities by speaking about them and then supporting those words with action. If we are to follow in His footsteps, we must embrace and pursue the same priorities to which He was committed. His mind was locked into the Kingdom of God; He even taught His followers: "Seek the Kingdom of God above all else, and live righteously, and he will give you everything you need" (Matthew 6:33).

What are the priorities that reflect our absolute sellout to the Kingdom of God?

> **Obedience to God.** "Anyone who obeys God's laws and teaches them will be called great in the Kingdom of Heaven" (MATTHEW 5:19).

> **Love.** "But I say, love your enemies! . . . If you love only those who love you, what reward is there for that?" (MATTHEW 5:44, 46).

> **Justice.** "God blesses those who hunger and thirst for justice, for they will be satisfied" (MATTHEW 5:6).

> **Peace.** "God blesses those who work for peace" (MATTHEW 5:9).

> **Holy living.** "Let your good deeds shine out for all to see, so that everyone will praise your heavenly Father" (MATTHEW 5:16).

> **Integrity.** "Just say a simple, 'Yes, I will,' or 'No, I won't'" (MATTHEW 5:37).

> **Generosity.** "When you give to someone in need, . . . give your gifts in private, and your Father, who sees everything, will reward you" (MATTHEW 6:2, 4).

> **Spiritual connection.** "You must worship the Lord your God and serve only him" (MATTHEW 4:10).

> **Spiritual wholeness.** "Is anything worth more than your soul?" (MATTHEW 16:26).

> **Biblical literacy.** "Haven't you read the Scriptures? . . .Your mistake is that you don't know the Scriptures" (MATTHEW 19:4; 22:29).

> **Faith in God.** "Because of your faith, it will happen. . . .
> You don't have enough faith. . . . If you had faith even as
> small as a mustard seed, . . . nothing would be
> impossible. . . . But with God, everything is possible"
> (MATTHEW 9:29; 17:20; 19:26).

> **Blessing people.** Jesus not only regularly taught this, but
> His constant healing of, training, and praying for others
> demonstrated how to bless them.

> **Disciple-making.** "Therefore, go and make disciples of all
> the nations" (MATTHEW 28:19).

Apparently, that's a life agenda worth dying for. . . .

His Character and Demeanor

The best intentions in the world get nowhere unless you
have the character and demeanor to carry out those dreams.
Once again, the nature of Christ deepens our understanding
of what type of person is capable of changing the world. In
His humanity, Jesus was able to develop the qualities that allowed Him to behave in revolutionary ways.

Are these same qualities evident in your life today? Are
you consciously refining these dimensions so that you will be
entrusted with greater responsibility for the advancement of
God's Kingdom?

> **Merciful and grace-giving.** "God blesses those who are
> merciful. . . . Do not judge others, and you will not be
> judged" (MATTHEW 5:7; 7:1).

> **Reconciliatory.** "Go and be reconciled" (MATTHEW 5:24).

- **Diligent.** "Keep on asking. . . . Keep on seeking. . . . Keep on knocking" (MATTHEW 7:7).
- **Teachable.** "Anyone who listens to my teaching and follows it is wise" (MATTHEW 7:24).
- **Courageous.** "Look, I am sending you out as sheep among wolves. . . . Don't be afraid of those who want to kill your body; they cannot touch your soul" (MATTHEW 10:16, 28).
- **Accepting.** "Anyone who does the will of my Father in heaven is my brother and sister and mother" (MATTHEW 12:50).
- **Surrendered.** "If any of you wants to be my follower, you must turn from your selfish ways, take up your cross, and follow me" (MATTHEW 16:24).
- **Repentant.** "I tell you the truth, unless you turn from your sins and become like little children, you will never get into the Kingdom of Heaven" (MATTHEW 18:3).
- **Humble.** "Those who exalt themselves will be humbled, and those who humble themselves will be exalted" (MATTHEW 23:12).
- **Servant-minded.** "But among you it will be different. Whoever wants to be a leader among you must be your servant, and whoever wants to be first among you must become your slave" (MATTHEW 20:26-27).

Many people were drawn to Jesus by His nature, without knowing much about what He stood for or His ultimate purpose. He wasn't a Revolutionary because He proposed a different philosophy. He was a Revolutionary because He lived differently, teaching a groundbreaking world order through

His demeanor and behavior. His words simply magnified and clarified what He was demonstrating in the flesh. One lesson we can derive from His life is that if you allow God to restore your spirit, then your life may follow.

chapter nine

› AMERICAN CHRISTIANS AS REVOLUTIONARIES

JESUS WAS THE ULTIMATE REVOLUTIONARY. We can learn how to be agents of life transformation for the Kingdom of God by understanding how He interpreted His role in life, how He established and pursued priorities, and the demeanor that facilitated His lifestyle and ministry. But we must also shed light on the philosophy that fueled His behavior.

In America, we tend to study passages of Scripture and draw general lifestyle principles. We interpret God's words to us through a particular analytic framework, one that is typically based on a synthesis of biblical teaching, cultural values, and familial training. But what happens if we apply a completely different framework? What if we read Scripture through the eyes of a Revolutionary? What are the seminal perspectives that the Lord divulged for us to integrate in our pursuit of a revolutionary life?

I encourage you to scour the Bible to create your own reservoir of insights into how Jesus, the Revolutionary, understood His journey. Here are a few of His perspectives that have shaped my view of what a revolutionary life is all about.

REVOLUTIONARY PERSPECTIVES

Live the Revolution

This revolution is not something you join; it's a way of life. Jesus made clear that the entrance fee for membership in this club is repentance, obedience, love, and service. To paraphrase Forrest Gump, "The Revolution is as Revolutionaries do." Most revolutions—American, French, Russian, digital, gay, civil rights, and others—gained ground for their cause by following a strategic plan. God's revolution, however, has no incremental plan. This war is won by the fanatics on God's side living in concert with the revolutionary ideals that Jesus prescribed.

This is a war that is not won by force. It is won by the daily demonstration of courageous faith—the faith to be God's person wherever He puts you, doing whatever He calls you to do.

Don't wait to sign up. Just live it.

Victory through Engagement

Most wars are decided in terms of territory seized or the number of enemies killed. Not this one. It is unlike any war ever waged. For starters, we already know who wins. Further, the most effective weapons are those that promote peace and understanding: prayer, love, blessing, and so forth.

And, of course, the war is ostensibly invisible, although it is waged in the material realm.

In fact, unlike all other wars, this one has no innocent by-standers. All are combatants who declare their side in the conflict through their words and actions. No gray area exists: you are either aligned with God, the champion of holiness and freedom, or Satan, the challenger promoting evil and enslavement.

Revolutionaries—the frontline warriors for the Kingdom—can claim victory simply by enlisting in the Lord's army. Embracing the role of Revolutionary and then perse-vering in the war does not guarantee victory—being a Revo-lutionary *is* victory. All we have to do is show up every day to fight for what's right. Like a fixed prizefight, the outcome has already been taken care of.

Motivated by Love and Obedience

But why, one might wonder, *should we bother to engage?* Why not sidestep the whole messy affair, and just lead a low-key, no-frills Christian life? Isn't it enough to love Jesus, accept salvation by grace, and then live however we wish until we reach heaven?

Well, for starters, there's that issue of bearing fruit. When Jesus told His followers, "Yes, just as you can identify a tree by its fruit, so you can identify people by their actions" (Matthew 7:20), He was intimating that all who receive the free gift of salvation ought to be so blown away by sheer grat-itude that they cannot do anything other than seek ways to change themselves and the world. Even though you cannot earn your way into God's eternal presence, your wise choices and good deeds become the evidence of your commitment and transformation.

And forget about fear as a motivator. Yes, we may harbor a healthy dose of fear due to the awesome power and unfathomable omniscience God possesses, but genuine Revolutionary zeal must be attributable to an intense desire to worship, thank, and serve God for His goodness and greatness.

In the end, we surrender our lives to serve Him out of love and obedience. He is the only One who matters in life. His incredible sacrifice for us causes us to do no less than give everything we have back to Him as our own sacrifice of praise and appreciation.

Marching Orders from God

Americans are used to controlling their lives. What makes Revolutionaries so bizarre is that they admit they do not have control of their lives and they are not seeking to attain control. Who else would you want controlling your life besides the God of Creation?

But admitting that we do not have control is only one step in the process of successful living. The other crucial component is to listen carefully so we get our cues from God. He seeks to direct us every step of the way. However, we must be sensitive enough to receive His direction. He speaks to us in various ways—through the Bible, wise counselors, direct revelation, signs—but all the communication in the world is meaningless if we are not attuned to His message and determined to obey His commands.

A Revolutionary knows who calls the shots, and he knows what the voice of the Commander in Chief sounds like. Success is not about proving our own ability by creating and implementing our own plans; it's all about our fervent desire to be used by God as He wills.

Leadership: Doing What's Right

A revolution is about changing what exists. Change requires leaders who intentionally introduce new direction. Every Revolutionary, whether positioned as a leader or not, fulfills a leadership role by virtue of affecting the lives of others who have ignored or resisted the truth of the Bible.

Whether you like it or not, being a Revolutionary means that at some point you will provide leadership to someone else. That's a privilege for which you must be ready.

One of the critical points of preparation is to make your choices based on what's right. Jesus criticized the leaders of His day for misleading people by making choices that were popular, easy, expected, personally profitable—but wrong. A godly leader—a true Revolutionary—does whatever is right, according to God's laws and principles. Even if the inevitable result will be resistance or persecution, Revolutionaries gladly bear any burden so long as their choices and actions honor God.

Internal Politics Are Absent

Jockeying for position occurs in most organizations, whether they operate under peaceful or wartime conditions. All the perks are up for grabs—titles, physical location, compensation, benefits, operational resources—and even the most committed players consciously grab for them.

Not so among Revolutionaries. No office politics exist because there is no office to rule, no official positions to win, and no "stuff" that matters. All that matters is pleasing the Boss. And that is accomplished by ignoring all of the usual goals in favor of being godly.

A Different Dimension

Do you get it? Being a Revolutionary is all about living life as a paradox. You win before you experience your initial skirmish. Faith triumphs over competence. Spiritual power overwhelms physical force. Humility generates attention and appreciation. Holiness defeats worldly cleverness. Those who surrender their lives defeat the enemy who seeks to destroy them.

Participating in this Revolution is not easy. Our enemy understands our objective and methods and will pull out the stops to counter our efforts. Just as victory comes through paradoxes, the performance of revolutionary tasks brings paradoxical results. Offering love will often inspire distrust and retribution. Serving those in need may trigger persecution by those being served. Living a simple life becomes exceedingly complex.

It does not matter. Focus. Be strong and courageous. You have already won. Now all you must do is persevere.

chapter ten

> HOW THE REVOLUTION SHAPES THE REVOLUTIONARY

HAVING STUDIED two dozen historical revolutions—political, religious, cultural, and professional—I find it apparent that individuals who participate in a revolution are radically changed by their immersion in the process. The ultimate success or failure of a revolution depends on how tightly its advocates align themselves with the cause—and how open they are to becoming the embodiment of what they profess to bring to life.

This is an important phenomenon: while change agents are probably drawn to a revolution to transform their world, their personal involvement in the process changes them in significant ways. They enter the fight for change holding a few compelling ideals, but they exit the process with a different view of themselves, as well as of the fundamental meaning and implications of the revolution. I would go so far as to say that sometimes their concern about recasting the world becomes not so much secondary as invisible. Their own journey has taken them to places they never imagined.

Typically, four highly significant changes appear to be produced by a revolutionary's investment in a revolution. Let me describe this metamorphosis in terms of the Revolution of faith that we are discussing in this book.

REALIGNING PERSONAL IDENTITY

Human behavior is a series of complex negotiations among our self-image, character, values, sense of purpose, and cultural parameters. Each choice we make is our best attempt to somehow balance the competing interests of those dimensions to optimize an outcome. Who we believe ourselves to be is a major determinant in our ability to be competent in our Revolutionary endeavors.

Your capacity to connect with God intimately and, therefore, to follow through on the challenges posed by the cause of Christ is inextricably bound to your self-image. Simply accepting Christ as Savior and having a respectful but casual relationship with Him do not give birth to a Revolutionary life.

To be a Revolutionary requires understanding the role of every human being within God's plan. You realize that you are a special creature in His universe—created for the purpose of knowing and loving God, reproducing additional lovers of God, and living in ways that reflect being made in

God's image and for His pleasure. Amazingly, we have been invited to be His partners in developing and advancing His Creation—minority partners, certainly; not so much peers as associates—and as such we can take heart in the fact that *we matter to God.*

We are valuable because God considers us to be so. We need not earn our stripes—in fact, He has made clear that we cannot earn status in His eyes, except through our relationship with His Son. Our worth stems from our commitment to loving and serving Him. Our relationship with God helps us comprehend the purpose of our life and defines the direction to pursue that will please Him and thus provide us with the greatest fulfillment.

Wrap your mind and heart around this realization: You are a slave to Christ, an ambassador of God, a servant of the King, a soldier in the invisible battle of purity and evil. You will find inner peace only when you know who you truly are. Only at that point can you be authentic. Joy escapes many believers because they don't fully grasp their identities as Revolutionaries; they labor in vain as halfhearted disciples. The emotional and spiritual ecstasy that Revolutionaries experience is linked to an awareness of their true role in the Kingdom of God. Until you become obsessed with imitating Christ and honoring God, your journey is moving in a dangerous direction. Devoting yourself to the Revolutionary way is a big step toward experiencing God's pleasure.

Let me also point out that a major reason why most local churches have little influence on the world is that their congregants do not experience this transformation in identity.

Our research indicates that churchgoers are more likely to see themselves as Americans, consumers, professionals, parents, and unique individuals than zealous disciples of Jesus Christ. Until that self-image is reoriented, churches will not have the capacity to change their world. After all, a revolution is a dangerous and demanding undertaking; it is not for the minimally committed.

CLARIFYING CORE BELIEFS

There is no room in a revolution for those who are ignorant of the foundational philosophy. These operations live or die on the vitality of their seminal ideas—ideas about truth, justice, value, freedom, and similarly weighty matters. God's Revolution is no different. The soldiers in this Revolutionary band must champion the breadth and profundity of the worldview God provides. By personally embracing those perspectives, their lives are altered.

Revolutionaries have a wholly biblical outlook on life, based on the belief that the Bible is God's perfect and reliable revelation designed to instruct and guide all people. The core beliefs of these Christ-followers relate to the existence, origins, character, and purposes of God; the origins and purpose of people; the need for and means to eternal salvation; the repository and content of moral and spiritual truth; and the existence, powers, and role of various spiritual beings. Possessing a biblical point of view on all of these matters, and allowing it to drive your moment-to-moment decisions, enables you to distinguish yourself from conventional thinking and behavior.

Know this: you become what you believe. Because your core spiritual convictions dramatically influence your life choices, your major spiritual beliefs shape your self-image and behavior. The Revolution, because it is based on applying biblical principles, constantly elevates and clarifies the central beliefs that facilitate sinners being transformed into forgiven, satisfying servants of the living God.

PART OF A COMMUNITY

Having a reference group as an anchor is important. Revolutionaries are often iconoclastic and frequently initiate their journey toward a new life with the intention of being fiercely independent rebels who will show the world how to do things the right way. Almost inevitably, these people discover three important things: they are not the only ones dissatisfied with the status quo, it is difficult to sustain their rebellion when they are alone in the process, and they are having less influence on their own than they expected. The result is for them to join forces, carefully but enthusiastically, with others who seem to be on the same wavelength.

Individuals involved in the Revolution of faith that is currently redefining the American Church are predisposed to communal activity. Why? They've been exposed to biblical teaching that emphasizes the relational nature of God and the connectional character of ministries. As much as they may appreciate the intensity and gutsiness of John the Baptist, they recognize that a solitary voice in the desert has less effect than a united voice in the marketplace. This is a major point of differentiation between social malcontents, who often act out their displeasure in isolated and unconstructive ways, and social reformers, who refuse to accept what is and agree to work in tandem with like-minded reformers to introduce needed transformation.

Integrating into a pool of compatible change agents has tangible benefits. Each Revolutionary's impact is multiplied by being part of a larger, harder-to-ignore group of compatriots. An individual's personal skills and gifts are exploited to maximum advantage, while the community compensates for each person's deficiencies. Affirmation from fellow transformers leads to increased strength, and being part of a larger force builds self-confidence. Both the cause and the individual are better off because of accountability in relation to thinking, message, behavior, and resource use. Revolutionaries take pride in their connection to the community of fellow zealots. As in any society, it is the community to which they belong that sustains them and nurtures them through the good times and the bad. This adopted community anchors them both to reality and to the idealism to which they aspire.

NEW FORMS OF BEHAVIOR

Modern life is an exercise in dealing with distractions. It has been argued that one reason Americans feel stressed, fatigued, and ineffective is that there are so many distractions in their day that they struggle to finish critical tasks, rarely focus completely on any specific pursuit, generally feel as if other choices might have been more satisfying, and compromise the quality of their performance by juggling so much simultaneous activity.

Intentional and strategic change—especially on a major scale—occurs because it has been tirelessly pushed through by believers with blinders. Revolutionaries' extreme resonance with the cause enables them to deny the multitude of distractions and seductions that could dissipate their effect. Sometimes these people are seen as narrow-minded or uninteresting because of their laser-like focus on Revolutionary ideals. Such negative characterizations are meaningless to the Revolutionaries. They receive their energy and their affirmation from God in ways that the world at large will never understand.

This disregard for the world's applause, combined with their intense dissatisfaction with the existing reality, enables Revolutionaries to act in ways that capture the attention of the complacent masses. The passion and intensity that cause them to do what they believe is right, oblivious to public reaction, are simultaneously intriguing and scary to those who uphold the white-bread norm. In fact, this public fascination with and resistance to Revolutionaries' behavior serve to spur the change agents on to ever more advanced forms of transformational activity.

A NEW PERSON

In the end, the Revolution may be more about reshaping the Revolutionary than it is about altering the course of society.

Revolutionaries themselves comprehend what is at stake and how critical it is to model transformation so others are more likely to buy into the process and its outcomes. The ultimate desire, of course, is to influence the world for Christ. But the means to accomplishing that lofty end is to be revolutionized by the Revolution.

chapter eleven

> THE MARKS OF A REVOLUTIONARY

JESUS' TEST OF A TRUE DISCIPLE was the fruit that ema-
nated from his or her life. He encountered numerous people
who talked a good game (such as the Pharisees), but He was
only enthusiastic about those who lived what they claimed to
believe. Over the past couple of years, as my research efforts
have concentrated more heavily on the emergence of the
Revolution, I have noticed that many people like to think—
and make others think—that they are Revolutionaries, but
their lives betray that deception.

How can you tell if someone is a Revolutionary? As Jesus
taught, you look for the fruit. But what are the relevant behaviors that support the verbal intimations? Again, the Bible
is the best source of such measures. I believe that not only
was the apostle Paul a stellar Revolutionary, but his letters to
the churches he mentored provide tremendous insight into
the distinguishing attributes of genuine Revolutionaries.

Paul's letter to the church in Rome stands out as perhaps
the most forthright commentary on what such change agents
look like. This is not surprising, since it would have taken ro-

bust faith to flourish as a Christian in the nucleus of the Roman Empire. There are great similarities between the contexts of the early Roman Church and the contemporary American body of believers. The apostle to the Gentiles offers guidance in seven areas of life: spiritual practices, personal faith, perspective on life, attitude, character, relationships, and behavior. (If you're willing, get your Bible and read Romans through in one sitting. That review will place the forthcoming ideas in a heartier spiritual context.)

SPIRITUAL PRACTICES

Paul's view of spiritual Revolutionaries is that they are *connected*: they have formed a deep bond with God and relate to people intimately because of that bond.

Paul highlights several specific practices for the early believers. Early in the letter, he underscores the importance of constant prayer and worship. Later on he reminds the Christians to pull out all the stops to get the Good News a fair hearing by everyone and to use the supernatural abilities God gave them for acts of service.

Recognizing that no one can anticipate everything that will come their way, Paul entreats Christ's devotees to remain sensitive to the Holy Spirit. His final exhortation regarding their spiritual practices is to do whatever they can to build up others' faith.

One of the lessons from this letter that I found most impressive was that Paul, like Jesus, was less concerned about religious ceremonies and completing a checklist of activities and events than he was about people being tuned in to God. Not once did he rant about being present at church every week or completing specified amounts of activity. His message was profoundly simple: stay in touch with God and follow your instructions as they are provided. It's all about deepening your relationship with God, not about consistently engaging in your routines.

PERSONAL FAITH

While Paul's key message on spiritual practices was to be connected to God, the overarching message Paul had for believers regarding the development of their personal faith was simply to *be available*. Available for what? Available to do whatever it takes to grow your faith stronger. Available to hear and respond to the Spirit of God. Available to see Him work through you because of your trust in Him.

Paul describes this accessibility another way by prompting believers to "give [themselves] completely to God" (Romans 6:13). He called disciples to surrender every dimension of their lives to God. Nothing shows your faith more irrefutably than your willingness to give away control and follow any directive given by your leader. Surrender is the proof of conviction.

PERSPECTIVE ON LIFE

Paul encouraged the early believers to be *firm and focused*. Focused on what? Producing fruit! As he wrote to the Roman disciples, "I want to work among you and see spiritual fruit" (Romans 1:13).

More particularly, Revolutionaries are urged to place their faith in God above all else, to be considerate of the needs of others and bless them whenever possible, and to be realistic in self-assessment. The bottom line in all of this: never lose confidence in your ability to make a lasting and positive difference in the world.

Bearing fruit is not easy. Paul does his best to describe the toughness of mind that a Revolutionary will need to make a difference. He challenges his protégés to turn a deaf ear to illegitimate criticism. He warns them that they will face hardships: trouble, calamity, persecution, hunger, poverty, and even death threats. And he cautions that God Himself may punish those He loves because of their offenses.

Revolutionaries are, indeed, a different breed of people. They accept the fact that life on earth is all about life after earth, and they live accordingly.

ATTITUDE

The attitude of a true Revolutionary is assured, appropriately righteous, and upbeat.

And why not? Who wouldn't feel secure knowing that they are connected to the omnipotent and omniscient God of the universe? That's why Paul tells Revolutionaries they ought to be confident and fearless.

And who wouldn't be righteous, realizing that their sole purpose is to obey God, based on the clear directives He has provided? When Paul admonishes the world-changers to hate evil, love goodness, and be patient, respectful, and forgiving (see Romans 12:9-21), that mind-set makes sense in the context of serving the Lord of truth.

And who wouldn't be upbeat about their existence, given the promises of the God they serve? Encouraging the body of Revolutionaries to remain happy and joyful isn't much of a stretch if you can stay focused on the big picture.

CHARACTER

Jesus majored on the character traits of His twelve disciples. Paul picks up the baton and drills home the evidence of revolutionary character. Integrity is a must-have quality: honesty, reliability, and trustworthiness are hallmarks he describes for the Romans. These characteristics make a change agent honorable.

Humility is a big issue for Revolutionaries. We have no grounds for arrogance; we are lowly sinners incapable of earning salvation according to the rules. Knowing who and what we are, in comparison to the standard set by Jesus, should help us stay realistic.

Empathy is another trait Paul singles out as crucial. If we are to be lovers of God and humankind, it will be hard to accomplish that goal without warmth and compassion.

RELATIONSHIPS

Revolutionaries are to be known by their *excessive love* for God and people. Once again, consistently following through on this is one tall order. How can we do it?

Paul recommends that we aggressively look for opportunities to bless people. He suggests that we strive for peace and harmony with them, which we can facilitate by avoiding senseless arguments. He also moves us to realize that we need each other for the fabric of the Kingdom to be complete (see Romans 12). A team player mentality fosters loving relationships, rather than competitive or jealous interaction.

It is important to see that Paul also highlights the special responsibility Revolutionaries have to each other. They are to seek unity with each other and always honor others. If we are to be the model for the world, what people see when they watch us together must reflect the affection and spiritual attachment we have for one another.

BEHAVIOR

The Revolutionary lifestyle might be summarized as *clean and productive*.

Look at what Paul writes about the transformational life. He calls the believers to holiness, for goodness' sake (see Romans 12:1). We know that God alone is holy and that Jesus' death and resurrection on our behalf give us the spiritual holiness to be with God in heaven, but in the meantime we are challenged to live an ever more pure and perfect life as evidence of our cooperation with the Holy Spirit who lives within us. Obedience to God's standards, motivated by our gratitude and desire to please Him, is crucial in this pursuit of the holy life. Paul points out that this effort should result in our being respectable representatives of the Kingdom.

The clean nature of our lives is certainly associated with how we think. We are prompted to scrutinize our thoughts in order to resist those that dishonor God. Revolutionaries are also encouraged to rely upon a "transformed" mind; because our actions flow from our thoughts, we must think like a transformed human being if we hope to act like one.

The changed mind of the Revolutionary will produce different lifestyle choices. Working hard, producing good deeds, and avoiding debt are examples of the productive life that emerges from an intense commitment to God.

THE CHECKLIST

Do you want to determine if someone is a Revolutionary? Look at the characteristics Paul lists in Romans, and compare them to the person in question. Even under the best of circumstances, you will never find a perfect, 100 percent match. But as you examine the life of a genuine Revolutionary, you will notice that he or she is different from the pack.

Did you notice the overlap between Paul's instructions and the spiritual passions of the Revolutionary? Paul hits them head-on: genuine worship, fearless outreach, consistent spiritual growth, wise investment of resources, opportunistic servanthood, and meaningful spiritual relationships.

How do you fare in relation to these attributes?

chapter twelve

> WHY THE REVOLUTION MATTERS

CHANGE IS A CONSTANT and unavoidable part of life. We endure changes and their personal implications every day—changes in technology, global politics, public policy, personal relationships, professional status, self-image, and more. Some of those changes happen to us; others happen because of us; all of them have some degree of influence on who we are and how we live.

Think about past revolutions and the effect they have had on the world. The Protestant revolution redefined faith: The religious authority structure was altered. The place of the Bible was radically changed, from a sacred book interpreted for the masses by professionals to God's personal words to the sinner. Worship became more intimate. The burden of responsibility for the breadth and depth of faith jumped from the local church to the individual. The Pope went from being the preeminent religious leader of planet Earth to the preeminent religious leader of the world's largest denomination.

More recently, the civil rights revolution (it was more than a movement) brought decades of struggle to a head. The self-image of blacks—and whites—was challenged and re-aligned. A new body of leaders arose to champion the cause and eventually implement its reforms. Society's resources and even its laws were significantly revised. New language was created to represent the changes introduced. The dreams and goals of black Americans were released from the bondage of racism.

The feminist revolution of the 1960s and 1970s refash-ioned the role of women in our culture. This shattered the notion that women were inherently suited to be stay-at-home mothers—incapable of holding a job, responsible for fulfilling the needs and desires of their husbands. It pro-duced new language about and for women. It identified and empowered a new band of leaders—women who cast a vision for a different understanding of, relationship with, and op-portunities for women. They facilitated these new ideas by motivating women to embrace this new philosophy of self, by investing resources to institutionalize these shifts, and by providing lasting guidance for their cause.

The Revolution of faith that is swelling within the soul of America is no different in scope. It will affect you and every-one you know. Every social institution will be affected. This is not simply a movement; it is a full-scale reengineering of the role of faith in personal lives, the religious community, and so-ciety at large.

THE SAME, BUT DIFFERENT

The burgeoning faith Revolution is markedly different from the two major faith revolutions that invaded American soil in the past.

The Great Awakening swept the nation from the 1730s through the 1760s. Like all successful revolutions, it provided new leaders, language, ideas, technologies, and structures. The Second Great Awakening, in the 1820s and 1830s, introduced similar realities. But the catalyst for both of these religious juntas was an emphasis on sin, the need for forgiveness, and the means to salvation. The ultimate product was the first-time spiritual conversion of sinners. The Great Awakenings were spiritual revivals in the truest sense.

The new Revolution differs in that its primary impetus is not salvation among the unrepentant but the personal renewal and recommitment of believers. The dominant catalyst is people's desperation for a genuine relationship with God. The renewal of that relationship spurs believers to participate in spreading the gospel. Rather than relying on a relative handful of inspired preachers to promote a national revival, the emerging Revolution is truly a grassroots explosion of commitment to God that will refine the Church and result in a natural and widespread immersion in outreach. This is the Church being restored so the Holy Spirit can work effectively through the body of Christ.

IMPACT ON BELIEVERS

As this transformational movement grows, sparked by the spiritual renewal of believers, Americans' faith experience and expression will be substantially altered. For instance, believers will not have an institution such as the local church to use as a crutch or excuse for wimpy faith. Each Revolutionary consents to be personally responsible for his or her spiritual state—whether that's growth or stagnation. Complaints about the pastor, church staff, programs, or other obstacles disappear from the conversation: the onus is now on the believer to put up or shut up. The failure to develop a robust spiritual life becomes the responsibility of the person God intended: you.

This shifting of responsibility will affect all dimensions of spirituality. Besides personal growth, believers will bear the obligation for performing acts of community service, promoting the gospel, growing their family in faith maturity, worshipping God regularly, developing intimacy with God, understanding and applying the content of the Scriptures, representing the Kingdom in all walks of life, investing every resource they manage for holy outcomes, and being connected to a community of God-loving people. No more waiting for others to do the job; every Revolutionary must handle the duty to *be* the Church with dedication and excellence.

This transition also means that believers will have a much wider base of options to choose from. The field of possibilities will no longer be restricted to what a congregation proposes, or what their denomination's agencies suggest. A global infrastructure of Revolutionary activities and alternatives will emerge, making plentiful choices accessible. Because the Revolution will naturally encourage people gifted in specific areas to produce ministry that exploits those gifts, the range and quality of options will expand the influence of the Church and each believer.

Expect children to be taken more seriously as spiritual beings. Revolutionaries have the duty to raise their family to be the Church of God. Instead of passing off their children to others in the hope that someone will do something that bears some fruit, Revolutionaries will accept God's challenge to raise each young one to become a spiritual champion. The breadth of the Revolution will make ample assistance available to satisfy that obligation without allowing these parents to abdicate their duty.

In the end, the Revolution transforms believers so that they can transform the world. Their perception of faith becomes more real and personal. Their relationship with God becomes more natural and intimate. The Bible becomes a true book of life-giving wisdom, indispensable for right and holy living. The very life of the believer becomes a means of worship and outreach. Tent-making—the practice of working at a non-religious job as a means of paying the bills while facilitating one's desire to be a genuine representative of Christ in the world—moves from a quirky, first-century idea to a defining, personal lifestyle.

IMPACT ON THE CHRISTIAN COMMUNITY

The Revolution will permanently alter the contours of the body of Christ in America. Of course, when a massive number of its constituency is transformed, the body itself is reshaped, by definition. But how the community sees itself, and how it performs its functions as a community, will change.

New leaders will gain recognition and authority among believers. Their role will not be building new institutions to replace the old. Rather, it will be providing guidance in the construction of new hearts and minds that produce a thriving Church community. Weaving together the spectrum of ideas, talents, and resources of believers into a richer ministry tapestry will be their challenge. Power, authority, and resources will be defined, awarded, recognized, and utilized in different ways as the Revolution matures.

The systems and structures that fostered the old Church will give way to new realities in the Revolution. New ministry organizations will emerge. Different educational methods and training systems will prosper. Technology will become more important in the networking and restructuring of the Church in its mission.

Whereas "Christian community" has generally been limited to the relationships facilitated within a congregation, the Revolution is bursting open the walls of the worldwide Church to birth a truly international network of relationships. The synergies resulting from this expanded horizon will be impossible to quantify—or contain.

Christians' broader view of the Church and of their own responsibilities will also bring forth a renaissance in global missions.

IMPACT ON LOCAL CHURCHES

Existing churches have a historic decision to make: to ignore the Revolution and continue business as usual, to invest energy in fighting the Revolution as an unbiblical advance, or to look for ways of retaining their identity while cooperating with the Revolution as a mark of unity and genuine ministry. My current research suggests the latter approach will be the least common.

For those congregations whose leaders choose either to ignore or fight the Revolution, the consequences are predictable. A percentage of them will be seriously impaired by the exodus of individuals—even though it may be just a few people leaving an already tiny congregation. Other churches will continue as if nothing new were happening in the faith world. However, every church, regardless of its public response to the Revolution, will feel increasing internal and external pressure to get more serious about ministry and to lock onto a vision from God for the congregation's existence.

The United States will see a reduction in the number of churches, as presently configured (i.e., congregational-formatted ministries). Church service attendance will decline as Christians devote their time to a wider array of spiritual events. Donations to churches will drop because millions of believers will invest their money in other ministry ventures. Churches' already limited political and cultural influence will diminish even further at the same time that Christians will exert greater influence through more disparate mechanisms. Fewer church programs will be sustained in favor of more communal experiences among Christians.

A declining number of professional clergy will receive a livable salary from their churches. Denominations will go through cutbacks, and executives will be relieved of their duties as their boards attempt to understand and halt the hemorrhaging.

To some, this will sound like the Great Fall of the Church. To Revolutionaries, it will be the Great Reawakening of the Church. New scenarios do not mean mayhem and dissipation. In this case, they represent a new day in which the Church can truly be the Church—different from what we know today, but more responsive to and reflective of God.

IMPACT ON AMERICAN CULTURE

Culture is the accumulation of behaviors and beliefs that characterize a group of people. It is comprised of the attitudes, symbols, language, rewards, expectations, customs, and values that define the experience and context of those people.

How will the Revolution affect American culture? No less dramatically than it will rehabilitate the Church. The most important change will be the heightened visibility of Christian activity by the ever-present Revolutionaries who are intent upon being the Church. They will affect the ways legislation is discussed and passed. They will model a moral lifestyle—and encourage others to follow suit. They will inject religious themes and ideas into conversations. They will restore dignity to the family as the cornerstone of a free, democratic, and healthy society.

New types of organizations will replace the inert stalwarts. Seminaries will be challenged to become relevant or move over. Christian colleges, secondary schools, and elementary schools will be challenged to be more overtly and pragmatically Christian in their endeavors. A more diverse continuum of service entities will blossom as believers seek ways to use their skills, money, and time in an effective and life-changing manner.

The Christian Church has effectively served as the scapegoat or whipping boy for the mass media for several decades. That will change as the Revolution makes it more difficult to target a Church that is so dispersed and so obsessed with holiness. The standard criticisms will ring hollow; the typical caricatures of Christian people will vanish as the skeptics and critics recognize a wave of change through which true love for others has replaced hypocrisy and infighting.

Even the economy will be impacted. Revolutionaries will move their peers with their commitment to hard work and excellence. The renowned Protestant work ethic, which has been replaced in recent years by a more lackadaisical, postmodern lifestyle ethic, will return with a third-millennium flavor. The consumer choices of Revolutionaries will instigate a new sector of the marketplace geared toward meeting their needs; existing entities that produce garbage antithetical to God's principles will face a serious fight for survival amidst the example and multidimensional attacks of the growing Revolutionary population.

THIS IS NOT UTOPIA

All of this might come off sounding as if all evil will be whisked away and only gentility, civility, love, and goodness will remain. Nothing could be further from the truth. Life will remain a war zone. Until Jesus Christ returns, the battle will rage on.

Revolutionaries will have an impact, but they will not dominate the culture—at least not in the foreseeable future. After all, they are sinners. They are and will always be imperfect creatures. They will fall prey to greed, lust, selfishness, and all the other vices and lures that Satan uses to undermine God's ways and His people. Conditions will get better, but this is not a return to the Garden of Eden.

Spiritual maturity is a process. En route to maturity, you can count on a lot of false starts and stumbling. Revolutions are famous for being messy: things rarely go as planned and are notoriously inefficient. I see no reason to expect this budding revolution of faith to be any different.

But that does not erase the phenomenal significance of this historic quest for more of God in American life. The world will never be the same.

chapter thirteen

> WHAT THE CRITICS WILL SAY

CHURCH HISTORIANS AND REVIVALISTS look back at the Great Awakening with envy. They admire the passion and perseverance of those who dedicated themselves to the spread of Christianity during the Colonial years. But they also remind us that a multitude of critics attacked the revival—especially from *within* the Church. George Whitefield, John Wesley, and other standard-bearers of the revival withstood harsh attacks from established churches who complained bitterly that the itinerants used unorthodox means of reaching people, disrupted the status and flow of existing ministries, threatened the stability of society, and undermined the security and authority of pastors and denominational executives. Today, however, we praise God that Whitefield and his colleagues persisted in thinking outside the box and enduring the unwarranted abuse from their spiritual kinfolk.

In fact, energetic resistance by the established church has accompanied *every* significant episode of growth in the Kingdom since the time of Christ. Jesus and His followers were slandered, ridiculed, physically abused, and murdered. The

111

Protestant Reformation produced heated debate and violent resistance. The Second Great Awakening drew strenuous opposition from the ecclesiastical community. Even the more recent and less extensive movements of faith, such as the Jesus Movement of the 1960s, were dismissed or attacked by religious leaders who were aghast at the different types of people, strategies, behaviors, and outcomes that characterized the freewheeling, hippie-friendly Jesus People.

The Revolution of faith that is emerging today is no different. If you mention that millions of deeply devout Christians whose lives are centered on knowing, loving, and serving God live independently of a local church, you can count on criticism from the church establishment. Being Kingdom-minded and seeking innovative ways of reaching the world and honoring God suddenly get redefined to mean that such efforts must be approved and controlled by the presiding rulers of the institutional authorities. Some of the same people who profess love to be their hallmark ruthlessly attack anything that threatens their interpretations or turf.

As you consider the heartbeat and role of the Revolution, here is what you may hear from mainstream religious leaders. Let me suggest a nonhysterical response.

CRITICS ARGUE THAT YOU MUST GO TO CHURCH

The major concern about the Revolution is that millions of its adherents are not affiliated with a local church. As described in earlier chapters, Revolutionaries' distancing themselves from formal congregations does not reflect a willingness to ignore God as much as a passion to deepen their connection to Him. In my experience, Revolutionaries do not try to draw other people away from the local church. Theirs is a personal choice based on a genuine desire to be holy and obedient, but finding that need better served outside the framework of congregational structures.

The Bible Says . . .

Mainstream leaders seem to be voicing three dimensions of concern about believers making a conscious decision to separate from the local church. The first is an appeal to their interpretation of Scripture. "To call yourself a believer but leave the local church is unbiblical," explained one angry pastor. "The Bible clearly teaches that we are not to forsake the assembling of believers to worship God. Scripture also commands us to be accountable to the church and to be under the headship of His anointed leaders. Jesus Christ established the local church. Abandoning it is displeasing to God."

That conversation—and several others like it—pushed me to return to the Bible to find out what God actually says about the Church. I discovered some interesting things. For instance, when the word *church* appears in the Bible, it refers to people who are "called out" from society to be the full expression of Jesus Christ on earth. That reminds me of what being a Revolutionary is all about: rejecting the norm and paying the cost to stand apart from the crowd to honor God.

In fact, when the Bible admonishes us to gather together, it does not imply that that should be a church service or congregational event. "And let us not neglect our meeting together, as some people do, but encourage one another, especially now that the day of his return is drawing near" (Hebrews 10:25). Such interaction could be in a worship service or at Starbucks; it might be satisfied through a Sunday school class or a dinner in a fellow believer's home. The same God who is more concerned about what's in our hearts than about mindless observance of meaningless routines refuses to impose specific regulations about our religious practices. He wants us to use the creative abilities He entrusted to us to express in our own way how much we love Him and want to glorify Him.

In fact, there is no verse in Scripture that links the concepts of worshipping God and a "church meeting." The Bible does not tell us that worship must happen in a church sanctuary and therefore we must be actively associated with a local church. It simply tells us that we must worship God regularly and purely, in spirit and truth. Take particular note of the fact that Jesus dismissed the organized worship of His day as "a farce" and intimated that we ought not be so limited as to how and when we worship God (see Mark 7:7). When the Samaritan woman asked about worship practices and places, Jesus responded bluntly that the place and even the form of worship meant less to God than the heart and commitment. He noted that, "The time is coming when it will no longer matter whether you worship the Father on this mountain or in Jerusalem. . . . But the time is coming—indeed it's here now—when true worshipers will worship the Father in spirit and in truth" (John 4:21-23). He was highlighting the same foolish irrelevancies that traditionalists argue about today.

We are commanded to worship God, and we are encouraged to meet with other Christians for various purposes. However, as we follow the development of the new covenant and the related community of faith, notice that Jesus and His disciples provide few guidelines and commands regarding such meetings. The same God who is so specific about things that matter to Him and that are important for us has provided few details about the logistics of Christian assemblies. That silence suggests that we have freedom to develop the means by which we act as a united body of disciples, as long as we perform the functions of God's chosen ones in ways that comply with His general guidelines of behavior and the functioning of the body of believers.

And let's be loving but honest about what really goes on within the body of Christ today. No informed Christian leader could make a straight-faced argument that involvement in a local church necessarily produces a more robust spiritual life than that seen among Revolutionaries. As seen in earlier chapters regarding the state of the Church in America these days, Christians who are involved in local churches are actually less likely than Revolutionaries to lead a biblical lifestyle.

We must also address one other reality: the Bible never describes "church" the way we have configured it. The Bible goes to great lengths to teach us principles for living and theology for understanding. However, it provides very little guidance in terms of the methods and structures we must use to make those principles and insights prevail in our lives. It seems that God really doesn't care how we honor and serve Him, as long as He is number one in our lives and our practices are consistent with His parameters. If a local church facilitates that kind of life, then it is good. And if a person is able to live a godly life outside of a congregation-based faith, then that, too, is good. Remember, Jesus looks at the fruit. "A good tree produces good fruit, and a bad tree produces bad fruit. A good tree can't produce bad fruit, and a bad tree can't produce good fruit" (Matthew 7:17-18).

True Revolutionaries agree that being isolated from other believers—i.e., the Church (note the capital *C*)—is unbiblical. However, while they may not be integrated into a formal church congregation, they are not isolated from the Church. They may not belong to a specific collection of saints that engages in routines and customs at a particular location and under the leadership of a specific individual or group. However, neither are they spiritual untouchables who have no connection to the global Church. Every Revolutionary I have interviewed described a network of Christians to whom he or she relates regularly and a portfolio of spiritual activities which he or she engages in on a regular basis. This schedule of relationships and ministry efforts is the Revolutionary equivalent of traditional congregational life—but better. These believers pursue the seven passions of a Christian Revolutionary with a variety of people, in different forms and environments, but they are exuberant about their faith life. Compared to the "average" Christian I encounter in our national surveys, I estimate that the "average" Revolutionary is substantially more Spirit-led, faith-focused, scripturally literate, and biblically obedient than their more traditional counterparts who are embedded within a congregation.

The New Church of Laodicea

The second stream of concern contends that believers will become spiritually lazy and even compromise the principles and theology of the Christian faith because of their disconnection from the local church. The problem with this argument is that we find a measurably greater degree of lukewarm faith among the believers in the pews. Revolutionaries, almost by definition, are zealous and passionate about obeying God's Word and honoring Him. More often than not, they resort to departing from a local church in order to foster that focus.

Warnings about heresy creeping into the minds and hearts of the Christian body are always worthy of consideration. However, it is just as easy to identify heretical teachings proposed from America's pulpits as it is to identify heretical Revolutionaries. After all, our research shows that only 51 percent of the pastors of Protestant churches have a biblical worldview! The embarrassing belief profile of Christians across the nation can be largely attributed to the quality of teaching they have received in sermons, Sunday school classes, and small groups. It is inappropriate to suggest that Revolutionaries are worse off because they do not receive teaching from a nearby congregation. In fact, we have learned that many Revolutionaries rely upon Bible teaching delivered through Christian media or via teaching of trusted Bible expositors whose recordings they subscribe to.

Revolutionaries are spiritual warriors. They do whatever it takes to lead a holy and growing Christian life. Because they are vitally concerned about the truths and principles they absorb, their media usage and organizational affiliations reflect the care they take to limit their exposure to that which is edifying. They are not perfect, by any means, but they are sensitive to the importance of exposure to people and information that will raise them to a higher standard, rather than drag them down to a defiling level.

Tearing Down the Institution

The final thread of dismay is based on the argument that massive departures from the local church will dissipate the hard-won, expensive resources of the church community and its influence upon culture.

As part of the Church, Revolutionaries have no interest in denigrating any segment of the Kingdom; their goal is to be agents of transformation who support and add value to the good that exists in the Church.

Again, from a practical standpoint, it is hard to take the "undermining church influence" argument seriously. Our research shows that local churches have virtually no influence in our culture. The seven dominant spheres of influence are movies, music, television, books, the Internet, law, and family. The second tier of influencers is comprised of entities such as schools, peers, newspapers, radio, and businesses. The local church appears among entities that have little or no influence on society. It seems that if Revolutionaries approach faith from a different angle, the Church has little to lose and much to gain.

To those who are worried about their investment in congregational real estate, the only answer is to recognize that the Kingdom of God is not about buildings and programs. Those resources can be useful in building up the body of Christ, but we can never allow bricks-and-mortar to be the engine that drives the Church.

FIVE REACTIONS TO THE REVOLUTION

Thus far, we have uncovered five distinct reactions to the Revolution.

The first—and at this moment, the largest of the groups—is those who are completely ignorant of the Revolution's emergence. As word gets out and the Revolution expands in numbers and influence, this segment will shrink considerably.

A second group is those who are antagonistic toward the Revolution. These individuals feel threatened by the extreme change represented by the seemingly unorthodox approach to spirituality. These individuals tend to believe (or to hide behind theological arguments contending) that the Bible disallows a believer to intentionally live at arm's length from the local church. The response of these folks ranges from outright hostility toward Revolutionaries, to genuine prayer that the wayward sons will return to a church home, to pity for these "backsliders."

A third group is the coexister segment. These are Christians who have adopted a "let them be" attitude, refusing to judge the spiritual journey of others. Often, these people search for ways to have a peaceful relationship with Revolutionaries and attempt to build bridges that facilitate continued harmony within the body of Christ. Most coexisters have little interest in becoming Revolutionaries, but they are willing to embrace them as brothers and sisters in Christ. Some of them will eventually join forces with the Revolution.

A fourth category is the late adopters. As in any situation where significant innovation is introduced, these people are nervously waiting on the sidelines for the transitions to become mainstream so it is safe to get on board. Because believers have a huge degree of confusion about life purpose and spiritual meaning and a latent desire to clarify such matters, this group will become a major feeder for the Revolution as time progresses. This group disdains risk. They will cast their lot with the Revolution once it seems socially acceptable and culturally unremarkable to do so. Whether their timidity will effectively remove the cutting edge of the Revolution or whether these pliable saints will be spiritually energized by the passion and focus of the Revolution remains to be seen.

The final category, of course, is the Revolutionaries. Millions of them attend church, and millions of others do not. But they all love Jesus Christ and are devoted to Him as their Lord and Savior. Knowing that they can be more effective lovers of God by recasting themselves as humble, single-minded servants, they are committed to the Revolution for the duration of the battle, willing to endure the criticism of fellow believers so that they can be the Church in the best way they know how. They are not so much interested in converting their detractors to be Revolutionaries as they are determined to honor God through their purity and passion for Him.

The agents of transformation I've spoken with realize that the only way to silence their critics is to be Christlike at all times. Even that did not stop Jesus' critics, and many Revolutionaries are resigned to the fact that perpetual criticism from Christians is simply an unfortunate and unjust price they will pay for loving and serving God with all their heart, mind, strength, and soul. Someday, they know, they will stand before the only true Judge and will be made whole by the One who reconciles everyone's accounts.

chapter fourteen

➤ THIS REVOLUTION'S FOR YOU!

I HOPE YOU HAVE GLEANED a few new insights into our culture and the Church from this book. Studying the Revolution has been a life-changing experience for me in many respects. It has stimulated my curiosity and restored my hope for the Christian body in America, redefined my beliefs about church and the Kingdom, and radically reshaped my spiritual habits. This book may not motivate you to become a Revolutionary, but I pray that it at least gives you a clearer understanding of what the Revolution is all about and how you can partner with the nation's Revolutionaries to advance God's Kingdom on earth. If this information strikes a deeper chord within you, then I pray that the book has provided you with the sense of value that Revolutionaries possess within the work of God's Kingdom. I hope that you claim the freedom to be whoever God made you to be in fulfilling your role in His service.

This is a great time to be alive—especially for those who love Jesus Christ. The opportunities to minister are unparalleled: the millions of searching hearts and agonized souls, combined with the abundance of resources Christians have at their disposal, make this a very special era for the Church. Throw in the rapid and profound cultural changes occurring, as well as the struggles local churches are undergoing, and we have an environment in which the birth of a spiritual revolution is inevitable. The confluence of those elements demands a dramatic response, and the emerging Revolution represents such a historic thrust.

There can be no turning back at this point, no return to the old ways and the comfortable forms. Although we cannot accurately predict what the Church will look like twenty years hence, we can be confident that it will be more different from than similar to the Church at the start of the twenty-first century. The Revolution is an extensive grassroots response to the undeniable and insatiable human longing for a genuine relationship with God our Father. The transformations it introduces are sometimes difficult to accept and oftentimes inefficient in their development, but the outgrowth is a stronger and more irresistible Church.

THE CHURCH YOU'VE ALWAYS WANTED

As you seek to comprehend the emerging Revolution and describe it to others, keep in mind its central facets. It is comprised of a demographically diverse group of people who are determined to let nothing stand in the way of an authentic and genuine experience with God. They are involved in a variety of activities and connections designed to satisfy a spiritual focus. They are God-lovers and joyfully obedient servants. They are willing to do whatever it takes to draw closer to God, to bond with Him, and to bring Him glory and pleasure. If that can be accomplished through existing structures and processes, they accept that; if not, they will blaze new trails to facilitate such a Spirit-driven life.

En route to this intimacy with God, they are integrating the seven spiritual passions of a true Revolutionary Christian into their lives. Their daily expressions of worship refine their sense of the beauty, the creativity, and the majesty of God. Their joy at knowing Him naturally provides the impetus to communicate to others the Good News about Jesus' sacrifice and offer of salvation. Their infatuation with the Kingdom fuels their consistent effort to know more about God's ways. They respond to His love by seeking ways to invest the resources they control or influence for Kingdom outcomes. Their friendships hinge on spiritual growth. They pursue opportunities to use their abilities to affect the quality of life in the world. And they recognize that their most important set of relationships is within their family and that Christ must be the centerpiece of their experience together. These passions enable Revolutionaries to remain centered on God in a world of distractions and seductions. Their attention to these passions allows them to *be* the Church.

At what stage, or under what conditions, is the Revolution successful? Revolutionaries recognize that spiritual success is more about surrender than results. They know that God examines the fruit of someone's life, but the real fruit of the Kingdom is flat-out, no-excuses obedience to God. Such submission produces a perpetual string of behaviors and outcomes that may be imperceptible to a frenetic and hard-hearted world, but represent major victories within the Kingdom. Why? Because life is war, and every time a soldier willingly engages in sacrificial battle for the King, His honor is advanced. Revolutionaries' complete and total surrender to Him and His cause *is* the essence of eternal victory.

It is this holistic devotion to being Christlike that triggers the transformational legacy of the Revolution. First, Revolutionaries are changed so profoundly that they see life through a completely different lens. Then, armed with that new perspective and the courage to respond, these individuals set about transforming the world by being replicas of Jesus in every space they inhabit.

The purity and authenticity of their cultivated spirit influence everything in their path. Their beliefs, identity, behavior, and relationships blend to project a persona that pricks the spirit in everyone around them. Analysts might say that the job of a Revolutionary is to reform the culture, but that confuses purpose and product. These extreme God-lovers reform the culture simply by being true representations of whom God made them to be. They do not create and enforce a carefully plotted and meticulously deployed agenda of reform. They simply live a holy and obedient life that a society suffering from the stranglehold of sin cannot ignore. The transformation that follows in their wake is not so much their doing as it is an inevitable result of God's creatures waking up to the difference between living in the freedom of Christ or in the shackles of Satan.

In past spiritual awakenings, dynamic preachers went

into society to bring people into a local church for further development. This era of spiritual growth is different. It features millions of individuals quietly using the weapons of faith that God has given them to be scions of transformation within the framework of their typical space and connections. The starting point is internal, not external: their message is their own transformation by Christ, made real in their words and deeds. Rather than draw people out of the world and into a relationship with an institution, Revolutionaries demonstrate what it means to be the presence of God wherever you are. This is a broad-based grassroots revival that has no single leader and no headquarters. The declaration of purpose is more than two thousand years old: the Bible.

In the great awakenings of America's history, the pattern was always the same: draw people into the local church for teaching and other experiences. In this new movement of God, the approach is the opposite: it entails drawing people away from reliance upon a local church into a deeper connection with and reliance upon God. In other words, past revivals were outside-inside phenomena, in which the dynamic and evangelistically gifted Spurgeons, Finneys, Wesleys, and Whitefields of the Church brought non-Christian people inside the local church to be ministered to. This edition is predominantly an outside-outside experience, where believers see the world as their church grounds and every human being they encounter as a soul to love into the permanent presence and experience of God. Many of these Revolutionaries are active members of a local church, but their primary ministry effect is not within the congregational framework but in the raw world.

THE AFFIRMATIONS OF A REVOLUTIONARY

What we believe drives what we do. What we believe matters to God—which is why so much of the Bible painstakingly explains God and His Kingdom (i.e., theology). The Revolution fosters a stunningly diverse array of activities that work together to produce spiritual and behavioral transformation. But Revolutionaries connect at the level of theology. What are the affirmations common to Revolutionaries?

I am a Revolutionary in the service of God Almighty. My life is not my own; I exist as a free person but have voluntarily become a slave to God. My role on earth is to live as a Revolutionary, committed to love, holiness, and advancing God's Kingdom. My life is not about me and my natural desires; it is all about knowing, loving, and serving God with all my heart, mind, strength, and soul. Therefore, I acknowledge the following:

> *I am a sinner, broken by my disobedience but restored by Jesus Christ in order to participate in good works that please God. I am not perfect; but Jesus Christ makes me righteous in God's eyes, and the Holy Spirit leads me toward greater holiness.*

> *God created me for His purposes. My desire as a Revolutionary is to fulfill those ends, and those ends alone. When I get out of bed each day, I do so for one purpose: to love, obey, and serve God and His people.*

> *Every breath I take is a declaration of war against Satan and a commitment to opposing him.*

> *God does not need me to fight His fight, but He invites me to allow Him to fight through me. It is my privilege to serve Him in that manner. I anticipate and will gladly endure*

various hardships as I serve God; for this is the price of participation in winning the spiritual war.

> *I do not need to save the world; Jesus Christ has already done that. I cannot transform the world, but I can allow God to use me to transform some part of it.*

> *My commitment to the Revolution of faith is sealed by my complete surrender to God's ways and His will. I will gratefully do what He asks of me simply because He loves me enough to ask. I gain my security, success, and significance through my surrender to Him.*

> *I am not called to attend or join a church. I am called to be the Church.*

> *Worship is not an event I attend or a process I observe; it is the lifestyle I lead.*

> *I do not give away 10 percent of my resources. I surrender 100 percent.*

> *God has given me natural abilities and supernatural abilities, all intended to advance His Kingdom. I will deploy those abilities for that purpose.*

> *The proof of my status as a Revolutionary is the love I show to God and people.*

> *There is strength in relationships; I am bound at a heart and soul level to other Revolutionaries, and I will bless believers whenever I have the chance.*

> *To achieve victory in the spiritual war in which we are immersed, there is nothing I must accomplish; I must simply follow Christ with everything I have.*

> *There is no greater calling than to know and serve God.*

> *The world is desperately seeking meaning and purpose. I will*

respond to that need with the Good News and meaningful service.

> *Absolute moral and spiritual truth exists, is knowable, and is intended for my life; it is accessible through the Bible.*

> *I want nothing more than to hear God say to me, "Well done, My good and faithful servant."*

Thank You, Lord God, for loving me, for saving me, for refining me, for blessing me, and for including me in the work of Your Kingdom. My life is Yours to use as You please. I love You.

➤ HOW A LOCAL CHURCH CAN RESPOND APPROPRIATELY TO THE REVOLUTION

ON FRIDAY I HAD LUNCH WITH GARY, a senior pastor whom I've known for several years. We have shared speaking platforms together and have come to appreciate each other. Over chicken sandwiches and sodas I described the Revolution and its implications for local churches. His response was warm and affirming.

"That's great," he exclaimed between bites. "Whatever it takes to get people to be God-focused. That's exciting stuff."

"I think so, too," I replied with some amazement. "Honestly, though, I'm a bit surprised by your reaction. Knowing that many Revolutionaries grow in their relationship with God outside the ministry of a local church, I was afraid you'd label me a heretic for advancing their cause."

"Hey, don't think it didn't cross my mind," Gary said as he laughed. "Besides, I've come to expect you to do anything you can to make my life tougher."

Gary paused, setting down his sandwich and wiping his fingers on a paper napkin.

"Truth is, I've been aware of what you're talking about for some time. I've watched various families that used to be in our church drop out and get involved in other forms of church life. So I realize that these Revolutionaries, as you call them, are not likely to return to our building, and that there are many others like them who are getting active spiritually but will never set foot in our church.

"But it shouldn't really matter," he continued quietly. "As a pastor, I've always wanted to help people become passionate, active believers—Revolutionaries. So it would be kind of hypocritical of me to get upset that people were becoming genuine disciples without my influence or outside of our church. God's Kingdom isn't about who gets credit. I should be as excited as you that these people are walking the walk. You know how frustrated I get over the legions in our churches that only talk the talk but ignore the walk."

"But Gary," I pushed forward, "let me play out the other side of this argument. If people in your congregation choose to grow outside of your ministry, then your attendance will drop. In turn, that means there will be less money in the offering basket, which then means your job will be in jeopardy. Your entire church body, which has been taught that numbers are the measure of impact, may lose their trust in you. That, of course, will be the start of your downfall. And besides," I smiled mischievously, "how could you face your colleagues at those pastor's conferences, tell them that your church has grown from two thousand to six hundred, and expect them to accept you as an equal?"

We laughed a bit uneasily before he chomped into another mouthful and answered. "I hear you. It's true. Our fraternity is very numbers conscious." Gary gazed at the ceiling for a few moments, reflecting on our dialogue, and then continued. "And I think you're right. I'm sure my elders would push back on any ministry strategy that did not produce better numbers. But you know as well as anyone—in fact, I think I heard you preach this at one of those pastor's conferences—that my job as a leader includes reshaping the way my congregation understands and personally experiences the Kingdom of God. In fact, I can envision a time when we aren't two thousand people and we are not growing numerically—but we are as healthy spiritually as we have ever been."

We both ripped into the final pieces of our meal. Gary stared at his cardboard plate and finished his thought. "I guess the bottom line for me is that I feel lousy about this because I can't win. I know that God won't judge my service as a pastor by the church's budget or attendance, but you're right: others will. So even if I have the Kingdom in mind and I'm able to move people closer to God, that victory will be irrelevant—or worse—to a lot of people if it does not translate into bodies in the pews."

We ate in silence for a few moments. I had no magic words to fix his dilemma; he was right. Finally, Gary shook his head and looked me in the eye. "But I guess none of that matters, does it? We're called to be faithful, not successful. What matters most is that each of us, working together as a community of people in love with Christ, does whatever we can to advance God's Kingdom. I need to please God. I need to teach and lead people in how to do that. I don't need credit, I don't need public recognition, and I don't need job security."

With a mischievous twinkle in his eye he added, "Just don't tell my wife that part about not needing job security."

The weekend passed and I thought a lot about what Gary had said. I was ecstatic that a young pastor of a large church was so enthusiastic about the Revolution. In my mind, he "got it." Maybe I was needlessly worrying about the reception the Revolution and Revolutionaries would receive from the institutional church. Maybe the Holy Spirit had been preparing the way more widely than I realized.

In a chipper mood, I arrived at a restaurant for lunch with another pastor friend on Monday, just seventy-two hours after my uplifting conversation with Gary. After addressing some ministry concerns that we had agreed to grapple with, I decided to test-drive the Revolution with my present colleague. An older pastor with a mid-sized congregation, Harry was a deep thinker and devoted churchman. I shared with him the same fundamentals of the Revolution that I had divulged to Gary three days earlier.

The reaction could not have been more collegial—or confrontational. Our scheduled ninety-minute luncheon turned into a three-and-a-half hour marathon in which I spent the last two hours on the receiving end of a lecture decrying the spiritual justification of the Revolution. Harry's closing volley summed up his position.

"So you see, George, God has no Plan B. The local church is God's Plan A, His chosen vehicle, and He does not need any other plan. Anything outside of that means is simply indefensible from a biblical standpoint. Never second-guess God, my friend. Follow Him and accept His paths. No church has ever been perfect, but that's no reason to abandon it. Remaking the Church into the form you desire, rather than the form God ordained, is simply not legitimate. Let God be God. Help the local church be more effective, but don't ever, *ever* take any steps to replace it."

I'm not waiting for Harry to buy a copy of this book. . . .

Clearly, the Revolution will be controversial. But as painful as such conflict may be, it is to be expected: all significant change stirs such tensions. As the Revolution unfolds, many churches and other ministries will struggle to adjust. What advice might help existing and future local churches to respond intelligently and strategically to the Revolution?

MAKE A CHOICE AND GET ON WITH LIFE

The biggest challenge may be the first decision you have to make about the Revolution. Right out of the blocks, you have to choose whether to fight against the Revolution or to encourage believers to become part of it. You can try to ignore it, but its growth in size and influence will eventually force you to choose one response or the other.

If you lean toward fighting it, why? You might do so to protect your turf, to protect the Kingdom of God, to protect biblical theology, or to protect the sanctity of your habits, traditions, and preferences. None of these motivations is worthy, however, in light of the fact that neither Scripture nor church history provides viable justification. God doesn't ask you to protect Him and His things; He can take care of Himself. He asks you to serve through love and obedience to His principles.

The only reasonable response is to somehow facilitate the radical commitment and life transformation that marks the existence of Revolutionaries. It is, after all, a movement of people who want more of God and are willing to do whatever it takes to make Him the center of their lives. These are people who want to be the Church. What spiritual body would want to resist, much less reject, such a group? Joining the Revolution does not mean forfeiting your congregational identity or church distinctives. It means acknowledging and advancing your bond with the universal Church and ratcheting up your commitment to serious Christianity. If you don't like the language—terms like Revolution, spiritual war, spiritual passions, and so forth—ignore the words and develop a dialect that fits your ministry culture. Don't get sidetracked by the peripherals; focus on the devotion to God and the 24/7 lifestyle changes that drive such a ministry.

The great leaders of the Bible recognized that effective leadership involved recognizing the presence of God and aligning themselves with whatever He chose to do. Face it, no matter how brilliant or devoted you are, you cannot fight God and win. The smart money is on those who recognize when and how God is at work and then grab on to His coattails. The emerging spiritual Revolution presents such a moment of spiritual opportunity. Why not see it for what it is and choose to participate in what God is doing?

BLENDING YOUR CHURCH AND THE REVOLUTION

How can your local church become part of the Revolution, to whatever degree is comfortable for its people and ministry? Here are four possibilities.

First, *learn from the Revolutionaries.* As humbling as that might seem at first blush, every God-honoring church and its leaders want to participate in ministry that breeds people who are God crazy. The thrust of this approach is to identify the points of strength in the Revolution and incorporate the heart of those dynamics into the ministry of the congregation. Whether the lessons relate to passionate worship, enthusiastic outreach, grateful and continual spiritual growth, energetic service, wise and generous stewardship, uplifting fellowship, or shared family experiences with God, there are undoubtedly insights into the spiritual life that your church could absorb from the Revolution. If your goal is to provide congregants with a faith experience that enables them to love, obey, and serve God, you won't be disturbed by the source that stimulates enhancements to your church's ministry.

Second, *seek ways in which your church can add value to the Revolution.* Remember, the Revolution is simply a collection of people obsessed with loving God to the hilt. They have needs that may be filled in a variety of ways—and perhaps your church's ministry can satisfy some of those needs. The local church is about ministry, regardless of who the beneficiaries may be. Because the Kingdom of God does not nurture or sustain any forms of internal competition, your church need not fret about helping people or groups grow at the expense of your congregation. Quite the contrary: Your congregation's existence can be justified only when it is blessing people, no matter where they hang their hat spiritually. Success in your church has nothing to do with membership or control, and everything to do with relationships and service.

Third, *reflect on what it means to belong to a church—your church.* Revolutionaries are spiritually minded, but they are also independent and fluid in their faith-building activity. They may wish to plug into your faith community for limited periods of time. Some might initially see such participation as selfish, but Revolutionaries' intention is usually to be a legitimate part of a community of believers—giving as well as taking, as opportunities allow. You must decide if yours is to be an open or closed faith community. If you are able to embrace the Revolutionaries without judgment, you are likely to find that they will add as much (or more) value to your church body as they extract. And, even if they did not, you will have the opportunity to bless those who are serious about their relationship with Christ and their service to the Kingdom.

Finally, *figure out how to create more Revolutionaries among those who are not aligned with the Christian faith community.* Your region is packed with people who are not focused on knowing, loving, and serving God. What a great challenge to your ministry! Whether you motivate them to connect with God within your congregational context or outside of it, your challenge is to raise up God-honoring people and get them into situations where they can love and be loved more deeply.

LEADERSHIP MATTERS

How a local church responds to the Revolution is primarily a leadership issue. If your perspective as a leader is to study the Revolution so you can combat and defeat it, you're missing the point of the Kingdom of God. It's not about protecting God from His people. It's not about protecting the territory you have been given. God does not need us protecting Him and His Kingdom: He desires us to be Kingdom-minded and open to following through on His plan for its advancement.

Worldly leadership principles are about conquering your foes and reaping the benefits of your skill and wisdom. Christian leadership is about listening to God and humbly following His lead, doing things that facilitate life transformation, and not worrying about the credit and applause.

The Revolution is not your enemy. Your enemies are

spiritual complacency that renders people vulnerable to negative influences, and the brittle wineskins that can no longer contain this extraordinary move of God in the hearts of His people. Love the Revolutionaries in your midst and remember that they are disciples who seek God with all of their heart, mind, strength, and soul. Don't be distracted by the routes they take in doing so. And be careful not to waste Kingdom resources fighting those same brothers and sisters in the Lord. If judgment is to come against the Revolution, it should not come from you. Your charge is to bless everyone with whom you have contact, and especially those who are your spiritual kinfolk in Jesus Christ.

BOOKS OF INTEREST

- Robert and Julia Banks, *The Church Comes Home*
  (PEABODY, MA: HENDRICKSON PUBLISHERS), 1998.
- Dietrich Bonhoeffer, *The Cost of Discipleship*
  (NEW YORK: TOUCHSTONE), 1995.
- Bob Briner, *Roaring Lambs*
  (GRAND RAPIDS: ZONDERVAN), 1993.
- Marva Dawn, *Truly the Community*
  (GRAND RAPIDS: EERDMANS PUBLISHING), 1992.
- Mike and Sue Dowgiewicz, *Restoring the Early Church*
  (ALPHARETTA, GA: ASLAN GROUP), 1996.
- Brian McLaren, *A New Kind of Christian*
  (SAN FRANCISCO: JOSSEY-BASS), 2001.
- H. Richard Niebuhr, *Christ and Culture*
  (SAN FRANCISCO: HARPER SAN FRANCISCO), 2001.
- James Rutz, *Megashift*
  (COLORADO SPRINGS: EMPOWERMENT PRESS), 2005.
- Dick Staub, *Too Christian, Too Pagan*
  (GRAND RAPIDS: ZONDERVAN), 2000.
- Leonard Sweet (editor), *The Church in Emerging Culture*
  (GRAND RAPIDS: ZONDERVAN), 2003.

WEB SITES OF INTEREST

- The Barna Group—www.barna.org
- BreakPoint—www.breakpoint.org
- Brewing Culture—www.brewingculture.org
- Josiah's Place—www.josiahsplace.com
- The Ooze—www.theooze.com

CONTACT REGARDING THE REVOLUTION

- revolution@barna.org

GEORGE BARNA has served in executive roles in politics, advertising, and marketing research, as well as pastoring and teaching at the college and seminary levels. He is currently the directing leader of The Barna Group. Located in Ventura, California, the company provides primary research (Barna Research Group); musical, visual, and digital media (BarnaFilms); printed resources (BarnaBooks); spiritual and leadership development for young people (The Josiah Corps); and church enhancement (Transformational Church Network).

To date, Barna has written more than three dozen books, predominantly in the areas of leadership, trends, spiritual development, and church health. Included among them are best sellers such as *Transforming Children into Spiritual Champions, The Frog in the Kettle, The Power of Vision,* and *User Friendly Churches.* Several of his books have received national awards. He writes a biweekly research report ("The Barna Update") published through his firm's Web site (www.barna.org). His work is frequently cited as an authoritative source by the media. He has been hailed as "the most quoted person in the Christian Church today" and is counted among its most influential leaders.

After graduating summa cum laude from Boston College, Barna earned two master's degrees from Rutgers University. He also received a doctorate from Dallas Baptist University. He lives with his wife, Nancy, and their two daughters, Samantha and Corban, in southern California. He enjoys spending time with his family, writing, reading novels, playing basketball and guitar, relaxing on the beach, and visiting bookstores.

George Barna can be reached at The Barna Group, 1957 Eastman Avenue, Ventura, CA 93003; or via e-mail at revolution@barna.org.